EMBASSY RESIDENCES
IN WASHINGTON, D.C.

EMBASSY RESIDENCES
IN WASHINGTON, D.C.

Direction, design and edition
BENJAMÍN VILLEGAS

General coordination and foreword
LUIS ALBERTO MORENO
GABRIELA FEBRES-CORDERO

Texts
LILY URDINOLA DE BIANCHI

Photography
ANTONIO CASTAÑEDA-BURAGLIA

Preface
WALTER L. CUTLER

English translation
PATRICIA CEPEDA

Villegas
editores

This book has been created, produced and published
in Colombia by VILLEGAS ASOCIADOS S. A.
Avenida 82 No. 11-50, Interior 3
Bogotá, D. C., Colombia
Telephone (57-1) 616 17 88
Fax (57-1) 616 00 20
e-mail: informacion@VillegasEditores.com

Complementary text
ODETTE MAGNET

Complementary photographs
Pages 18, 20, 21, 22, 23, 24/25
ISABEL CUTLER

Copy editing
ALEJANDRA CEPEDA O'LEARY

Art Department
HAIDY GARCÍA

First edition
September 2003

ISBN
958-8156-13-0

Front Jacket, Embassy of Colombia
Back Jacket, Embassy of Turkey
Page 1, Embassy of Indonesia
Pages 2/3, Embassy of Russia
Page 4, Embassy of Brazil
Page 7, Embassy of Kuwait
Page 8, Embassy of Germany
Page 11, Embassy of Chile

VillegasEditores.com

CONTENTS

FROM THE PUBLISHER

Benjamín Villegas

This book is a tribute to the cultural and architectural heritage enshrined in the embassy houses of Washington, D.C. It may be seen as an expression of Colombia's admiration and respect for the proud capital of the country to which it renders homage, a world center whose assembly of embassies and diplomatic missions represents a perfect example of the ideal of peaceful co-existence, or at least a sincere effort to live up to it.

It is also a tribute, by the Colombian Embassy, to the diplomatic missions that occupy these homes, not only for conserving their splendid architecture and decor but also for the generous way in which they have cooperated with their colleagues from our Embassy, proudly opening their doors to the reader and allowing him to see treasures which are rarely shown to the general public.

Through this privileged access, the reader also has the opportunity to learn about the history of these houses and of the diplomatic life of that great nation's capital.

This is a major achievement, because these residences and embassies are not open to the public: you may only enter them by special invitation. Tourists and visitors to Washington, D.C., have to be content with their external aspect – a distant glimpse, through grilles and gates, of their imposing façades, ornate state rooms and splendid gardens. The embassy houses are, in a way, one of the best-kept secrets of Washington, D.C.

It is a pity, because many of these embassy residences are living examples, never to be repeated, of the best of early-20th century U.S. architecture. Others, like the recently-finished German embassy, are daring expressions of contemporary architecture, or noteworthy reinterpretations of traditional styles, like that of Korea.

These houses also form a delicious patchwork quilt of artworks and furnishings from all over the world and of reminiscences of the famous personalities who have lived and worked in them. Each country takes care to show the best of its heritage, history and culture in its embassy residence.

Indeed, it would be hard to find, in other parts of the world, a center of power that is more attractive or more suitable for displaying the unique treasures of the many different countries which are represented there.

Finally, this book is an impressive example of the achievements of Colombian talent, a tribute to the professionalism, team-work and enthusiasm of our Ambassadors in Washington, the editor and director of the project, the author of the texts, the photographer and the translator.

 For all of these reasons, this book is fascinating, beautiful and a delight to read. For us, this is a motive of pride and excitement.

FOREWORD

Luis Alberto Moreno, Gabriela Febres-Cordero

When you visit the Singapore Embassy residence, your eye travels from the grand Persian rug to the aluminum relief by the Singaporean artist, Sim Kern Teck, over the chimney, then it comes back and stops at the perfect Chinese Han dynasty head of a horse at the center of the table.

Washington is a city of timeless ideals embodied and expressed in the nearly timeless stone and marble of world-famous monuments. The White House, the Lincoln and Jefferson Memorials, the majestic dome of the Capitol – they are as familiar to us as the Eiffel Tower, the Tower of London, St. Peter's, or the Taj Mahal. But the great buildings of Washington speak as few others anywhere else do of the history and the hope that has summoned this nation and the world to the dream of "liberty and justice for all".At the dawn of the 21st century, the Pilgrim promise of three centuries ago unfolds in this "shining city, the eyes of all people upon it". Because it is the center of the world's preeminent political and economic power, decisions made here, along the banks of the Potomac River, are felt in the most remote villages of every country and continent, shaping a new world and a new future for generations to come. All who look to the United States pray that it may be guided now and always by the noble words inscribed in those monuments, and by the spirit that raised them up against the sky.

But the Washington that is in so many ways at the center of the nation and the world also expresses its living heart and soul in countless places beyond these great public sites. To truly know this marvelous city, you have to explore its winding foot paths, its open green parkland, its ethnic neighborhoods and restaurants, its stunning art galleries and increasingly rich cultural life – and often less noticed, but powerfully revealing and important, its diplomatic life. Yet unlike almost everything else in Washington, the embassy residences are closed to the public. Behind the closed doors are found not just the comings and goings of negotiations and the grit of policy making, but the artistic and architectural expression of the heritage and culture of a hundred other nations. For example, in countless details, large and small, the Colombian Embassy expresses the spirit of Colombia, never more so than when it exhibited the works of our great sculptor Fernando Botero. This book opens the closed doors of forty-one embassy residences, displaying for the first time their diverse beauty and the wide range of their different visions.

The art of diplomacy, as old as civilization itself, is a complex mixture of political, cultural, economic and social elements. As an official emissary, the ambassador represents far more than a government and its foreign policy. In our own experience, and that of many of our colleagues, the work of diplomacy reaches beyond issues like tariffs and trade, arms control, social progress – or even the common cause of defeating terrorism. The larger challenge is to widen knowledge and understanding of the land from which we come, something best done in the more intimate and informal setting of a private residence.

And so here lies the importance, often unsung, of the spouse. An embassy residence must be a home for a family as well as the symbol of a nation, and that is no easy task. It is not just a place for the explicit making of policy; it must also be a showcase for artists and businessmen, for writers and politicians, for journalists and heads of state.

And this, too, is statecraft, and requires a subtle touch. Tribute to such work is, we believe, long overdue, and this book captures that other side of diplomatic life better than any other we have seen. Here in these pages fabled Embassy Row comes to life as never before.

This extraordinary book is the brainchild of Benjamín Villegas, founder of Villegas Editores in Bogotá, who has won a worldwide reputation as the publisher of books as lush and exquisite and unique as his homeland, Colombia. Benjamín Villegas has an amazing gift for seeing a book in its totality while it is still only an idea. All Colombians are blessed by his contribution, and we are honored that he asked us to write this introduction. As you turn these pages, you will unquestionably agree with his choice of the photographer, our fellow countryman Antonio Castañeda.

This book would not have been possible without the collaboration of the diplomats who are fortunate enough to live in the forty-one embassy residences profiled here. We are grateful that so many of our fellow diplomats opened their doors and their hearts to this project.

That, to us, is the singular appeal of this book. It opens doors – many doors, in fact, both literally and figuratively – to an aspect of Washington that so very few ever have the chance to see up close. It is a privilege to present to you, the reader, a rare glimpse into some of the most lovely homes in America: homes that have borne witness to history, entertained presidents, kings and queens, and seen former enemies shake hands and break bread. What happens within these walls goes far beyond them. The embassy residences of Washington are indeed monuments of their own special kind, living and breathing testaments to our interconnected world, buildings worthy of this wonderful city and all it stands for, a place we have been honored to call our second home for the past five years during a decisive time in our own country's history.

So welcome to these homes, a very special part of Washington's life and the world's.

The imposing Oval Salon of the Argentinean Chancery – painted in three different tones of gold – possesses the dimensions of the pampas: one hundred dancers could glide across the parquet floors in a tango contest without bumping into each other. In the middle of the room stands the marble chimney. Eight curved banquettes, specially commissioned, follow the contours of the room.

PREFACE

Walter L. Cutler, text
Isabel Cutler, photographs

Loggia, Meridian House.

The practice of diplomacy takes many different forms, extending broadly from formal negotiations in conference halls and discussions at foreign ministries to office calls at chanceries and a range of written diplomatic communications. Business can also be transacted by being "drawn aside" by one's interlocuteur at a social gathering or through informal chats on the golf course. But over the course of more than thirty years as an American diplomat, I learned how very valuable a "home setting" can be for developing the mutual confidence and comfort that underlie truly effective diplomatic intercourse. And therein lies the classic importance of the Ambassador's Residence.

The Residence is where the Ambassador and his or her spouse carry on representational activities surrounded by décor, architecture and even landscaping that reflect their country's distinctive culture. More often than not, rooms are sufficiently spacious to accommodate the large receptions and dinner parties that are staples of diplomatic life. It is sometimes challenging, however, to find or make in such grand and stately Residences the warm, home-like atmosphere – that small room or even an alcove – where in my experience the most valuable diplomatic discourse is often conducted. In Residences where there is a clear division between the formal representational rooms on the one hand, and the more informal family quarters on the other, I have found that inviting one's guest into the latter can be an effective way to develop the familiarity and friendship so important to productive personal diplomacy.

Having been the host at functions in U.S. diplomatic Residences around the world, more recently as President of Meridian International Center I have enjoyed being the guest of many of the 175 foreign Ambassadors accredited to Washington. As depicted so magnificently in the following pages, their residences range widely in size, age and design. But, as in all countries, it is in these varied structures that the world's diplomats, by making their houses into homes, by combining the professional with the personal, not only enhance their own impact on global affairs, but also contribute a rich cultural and social dimension to life in our nation's capital.

It is appropriate that Meridian International Center, dedicated to promoting global understanding and working closely with Washington's diplomatic corps, is headquartered in two of the capital's most beautiful mansions built on the city's Meridian Hill by former American ambassadors. One, Henry White, had been ambassador to Italy and France; the other, Irwin Laughlin, had served as minister to Greece and ambassador to Spain. Both houses were creations of the noted architect John Russell Pope, who also designed the Jefferson Memorial, The National Gallery of Art, and many grand residences including that of the Brazilian ambassador.

The two retired envoys filled their side-by-side dream homes with European and Asian antiques and their beautiful gardens with ornate trees and statuary. Nearby were the Residences of several foreign ambassadors, including those from France, Poland, Spain, Italy and Mexico.

Left
*Front entrance
Meridian House.*

Opposite page
*Front entrance
White Meyer House.*

Dining room,
White Meyer House.

Today, long after ambassadors White and Laughlin have passed on and their progeny have moved away, these stately mansions continue to provide a welcoming and appropriate venue for foreign diplomats assigned to Washington and for thousands of others who each year come from countries all over the world for to meet with their American colleagues. At the same time, it is in Meridian's mansions where Americans seek knowledge and understanding of other countries and cultures through seminars, briefings and conferences in which many foreign ambassadors assigned to Washington play an active role. Each October, some 30-40 ambassadors support Meridian's activities by hosting formal dinners in their respective residences before gathering with other guests in

View of loggia front entry hall, Meridian House.

Meridian's festively decorated houses for what has become one of the capital's premier social events: the annual Meridian Ball.

I have often thought how pleased the good ambassadors White and Laughlin would be to know that, today, the spacious rooms and magnificent grounds of their former homes continue to serve as a place "where the world comes together" to strengthen mutual understanding. And they would also be pleased to know that, while several embassies have over the years relocated to more spacious and modern facilities elsewhere in the capital, others have remained and continue to lend a distinctive diplomatic air to historic Meridian Hill.

Meridian House with the U.S. Capitol and Washington Monument in background.

Pages 26/27
The south façade of the embassy residence of the United Kingdom, with the double colonnaded portico built of Indiana limestone, is intended as a specific reference to the traditional Virginia plantation house, and leads to the Rose Garden.

INTRODUCTION

Jane C. Loeffler, Ph. D.

There is something magical about entering an embassy residence. It is like being instantly transported to a faraway place. And that is precisely how it should be, because an embassy represents a foreign country, and the ambassador's residence is supposed to feel like home. With embassies from 175 nations, Washington, D.C., is unique among American cities. In fact, the presence of a large and cosmopolitan international community plays a key role in defining the identity of the nation's capital. There may be consular offices and special missions in Boston, New York, San Francisco, and other cities across the country, but embassies are located only in the capital, the seat of the federal government and home to the American president.

As the highest-ranking diplomats, ambassadors head delegations that vary in size from several individuals to hundreds. The delegations consist of political and economic advisors, consular officers, cultural attachés, and an array of others, including military and trade missions, and support staff. An embassy is the entity comprised of all these individuals along with their workplaces and official residences. Usually, the only official residence is the ambassador's house, known as the embassy residence. It can also be referred to simply as "the embassy." Confusion arises when the same term is used to describe the office building. To distinguish the two building types, embassy office buildings are known as chanceries.

Unlike chanceries, which are "public" buildings because they serve a public constituency, embassy residences are private. Like any homes, they welcome only invited guests. But they are no less significant to diplomacy. In fact, some may argue that what goes on at a reception or dinner party at an ambassador's residence is equal in importance to what takes place at a chancery. A residence provides an informal setting in which diplomats can mix and mingle with one another and with high level U.S. government officials, business and civic leaders, educators, cultural figures, and local residents. The format may be entertainment, but the business is serious – promoting cross-cultural communication, trade, and national identity.

When the Prime Minister of Denmark visits Washington, for example, the Danish ambassador can introduce him to officials from the White House, the State Department, the Pentagon, and representatives from Capitol Hill in the intimacy of his own elegant residence, a house designed in 1960 by Danish architect Vilhelm Lauritzen. Such an evening offers guests a chance meet and visit in an "unofficial" way. If the guests happen to notice the state-of-the-art Bang and Olufsen television or the CD player that opens automatically as you approach it, so much the better, because Bang and Olufsen is a major Danish electronics firm. If they happen to admire the modern and antique furnishings, that is also a plus, because they are all Danish, as is the art on the walls. Even the food, prepared by the Danish chef, features Danish culinary specialties. In this way, guests literally taste the flavor of Denmark and acquire an awareness of a place they may never have visited while making personal and professional connections that may prove useful.

Other ambassadors host similar events all the time – using hospitality to create good-will. That is the reason, for example, why the Italian ambassador and his wife have used their spacious gardens as a site for a barbecue to help raise funds for medical research that benefits Washington-area children, why the Brazilian ambassador and his wife have entertained judges and alumni of leading U.S. law schools, and why the Belgian ambassador and his wife have hosted dinners for patrons of the Washington Opera. It is also why the Colombian ambassador and his wife have raised funds to support educational opportunities for disadvantaged Latino youths and art programs for senior citizens, and why they have helped endow music education programs in the D.C. public schools by hosting the National Symphony Ball. In addition, the Embassy annually donates more than 50 000 roses from Colombia to an array of charitable events. By extending a welcome to the Washington community and by finding ways to facilitate face-to-face contact between themselves and Americans, ambassadors in Washington make friends and further the interests of their own countries.

Even in the age of telecommunications, being in the right place is essential. When a country is known through the way it presents itself to the public, the appearance of its buildings is part of its mission. To paraphrase President Grover Cleveland, who lobbied Congress in 1896 (unsuccessfully) to purchase the first official residences for American diplomats, "shabbiness" is incompatible with a proper diplomatic dwelling. As this volume illustrates, foreign diplomats have heeded that advice. Their houses in Washington are anything but shabby. To the contrary, they are beautifully furnished and impressively

The Neo-Classical Revival embassy residence of The Netherlands dates from 1929 and was designed by the Washington architect Ward Brown at the request of the original owner, Louis Septimus Ownsley, "the Baron of Traction." It was purchased in 1944 by the Dutch government.

Pages 32/33
The words of the architect, O. M. Ungers fully apply to the German Embassy: "…the residence of the ambassadors should not only serve a functional purpose, although functionality is not to be underestimated. It is a visual testimony of a nation's technological standards and artistic achievements. In this respect it is not a normal private house, but rather an official residence."

maintained because they are recognized symbols of national identity in a city where symbols really matter.

Originally, the head of a diplomatic delegation lived and worked in a single building, often a house or apartment he leased himself for that purpose. For example, when John Adams arrived in London in 1785 as the first American minister to the Court of St. James, he rented a brick house on Grosvenor Square for his family and his small staff. Similarly, the first delegations to Washington rented modest quarters in the newly established capital. Little more than a squalid settlement, the city must have seemed like a rustic outpost to diplomats from London and Paris and other places with long and illustrious histories and grand architectural traditions.

To his credit, Pierre Charles L'Enfant envisioned a powerful city when he laid out the plan for the new capital in 1791. He even designated an area adjacent to the Mall for a row of palatial houses for representatives of foreign countries. By building impressive houses near the White House and the Capitol, he thought, foreign governments would

add legitimacy to the new nation. As it turned out, foreign governments did not build new buildings for themselves at that time, but L'Enfant perfectly understood the power of proximity. In the two hundred years since he drew up his plan, the foreign presence in Washington has grown steadily and embassy residences and chanceries have congregated as near as possible to the White House and the nexus of power that it represents.

There were few foreign representatives in Washington in the years when the United States was a young nation struggling to establish itself. When the country sent its first diplomatic emissaries to France, the Netherlands, Great Britain, Russia, and Spain, it welcomed emissaries from those countries in return. By the early years of the nineteenth century, Washington had exchanged envoys with some two dozen countries, including Brazil, Chile, Colombia, Venezuela, Denmark, Belgium, and Turkey. By 1843, the first U.S. diplomats were accredited to China.

Greece, Japan, Romania, and Korea were among the nations that sent representatives to Washington during the nineteenth century as the United States expanded its involvement in the international community. In accordance with America's antipathy for pomp and elitist tradition, what President Cleveland called "unnecessary glitter and show," all diplomatic delegations until that time were headed by low-ranking diplomats – chargés d'affaires, envoys, or ministers whose quarters were officially known as legations. In 1893, Cleveland appointed Thomas F. Bayard Ambassador Extraordinary and Plenipotentiary to the Court of St. James, the first American diplomat to hold that title. Similar appointments to France, Germany, and Italy put the United States in the diplomatic company of the world's major powers for the first time. Those nations elevated their emissaries to the rank of ambassador and established the first embassies in Washington.

Below, left
The mansion which houses the Chilean Embassy residence, with its Louis XV façade, was built in 1909 by Nathan Wyeth, one of the most sought-after architects of the era. He designed the West Wing of the White House, the current Russian Embassy and the Key and Tidal Basin Bridges. He built the home for his cousin, the rich widow Sara Wyeth. The residence was bought by the Government of Chile in 1923 and since then its flag waves from the sunny balcony of the second-floor sitting room.

Below, right
This mansion, which formerly housed the Mexican Embassy residence, was the luxurious MacVeagh Palace until 1921, when it was purchased by the government of Mexico and became the home of its representatives. In 1990 it was turned into the spectacular Mexican Cultural Institute, one of the true jewels of the city.

In 1913, Czar Nicholas II purchased what is now the Russian Embassy Residence, which was then known as the Pullman mansion. The original owner was Hattie Pullman, the widow of the sleeping-car magnate, who had it built as a gift for her daughter and her congressman son-in-law.

Many of the elegant houses that now serve as ambassadors' residences and chanceries were not originally built by foreign governments for embassy use. Instead, they were constructed by self-made millionaires who flocked to town at the turn of the century to hobnob with the politically powerful and to dabble in public service. (There were also those who sought access to the diplomatic community so their daughters might meet and marry the young noblemen who occasionally served as diplomats.) Often shunned by polite society elsewhere, these newly minted moguls were determined to see and be seen. They were welcome in Washington, so much a city of transients. Even with their huge new houses, their presence was only seasonal, however. Most of them owned and maintained other houses elsewhere. The new houses were simply settings designed for entertainment and temporary residence.

Thomas F. Walsh, who made his fortune in the gold mines of Nevada, was among the first of the tycoons to establish himself in Washington with a fifty-room house on Massachusetts Avenue, just above Dupont Circle at the edge of the developed city. The environs were semi-rural when Walsh commissioned architect Henry Andersen to design a house that suitably expressed his social ambition. He spent more than $830 000 to build it and millions to furnish it in 1902, when those sums represented a vast expenditure, approximately $17 million in today's dollars. Two years later, distiller Thomas T. Gaff arrived from Cincinnati and moved into a mansion designed in the French style by Jules Henri de Sibour

Above, left
*The Norwegian Embassy
residence. Originally built in
1931 to house both offices
and living quarters for the
chief of mission, today it is
the Ambassador's residence.
The new chancery –built in
1978– is around the corner.*

Above, right
*The Holy See is considered
the crowning achievement
of the American architect
Frederick Vernon Murphy. It
started as a Roman palace in
the first drafts and later
turned into a very modern
building for its time,
very much in tune with the
industrial architecture of the
thirties. Murphy started
work as soon as the land
was acquired in 1931; but
the residence was only
finished in 1939.*

Opposite page
Marhaba, *the word for
"welcome" in Tunisia, has
been the motto of the
residence of the Tunisian
ambassadors since the home
was purchased in 1956.
The building's first owner
had lived in Portugal and
had a home built in the
Mediterranean style to
please his daughter.*

a block away. In 1906, another mining magnate, Hennen Jennings, selected a site slightly west of Walsh's at Sheridan Circle, and George Oakley Totten, Jr., designed him a handsome classical revival palazzo. Edward Everett, whose millions came in part from his invention of the crimped metal bottle cap, established himself in 1914 across Sheridan Circle in a house that featured a potpourri of styles – Italian for the ballroom, English for the dining room, and French for the drawing room. Everett's architect was also Totten. It was not long before Massachusetts Avenue and adjacent streets were lined by lavishly appointed new houses and the neighborhood known as Kalorama boasted the liveliest social scene in town.

But Kalorama was not the only hot real estate in town. Upper Sixteenth Street at the top of Meridian Hill was another. There, about two miles due north of the White House and distant from the built-up part of the city, former Missouri senator John Henderson and his wife Mary had built themselves a rusticated stone manse in 1888. From their colossal villa, the Hendersons had view over the city and a vista leading directly to the president's house. Mrs. Henderson envisioned an exclusive hilltop community that included prominent government buildings, memorials, and foreign embassies. To that end, she acquired dozens of sites, hired architects, and set about the business of attracting buyers.

In 1907, Mrs. Henderson retained Totten, who had just completed the Jennings House, to design a house for the French ambassador at 2460 Sixteenth Street. Nearby at 2640 Sixteenth Street, Totten designed a house that Mrs. Henderson sold to the Polish government in 1919, and just north of that, he designed a white stone mansion that Mrs.

The lovely home which houses the residence of the Bolivian ambassador has been the property of the Bolivian government since 1941. Built at the beginning of the last century, it was originally known as the "White Mansion", after its first owner, Senator White. But the name may also have come from the color of the façade.

Henderson offered to the U.S. government as a permanent residence for the Vice-President. She may have been a forward-thinker, but her offer was refused. That palatial house was purchased by Spain as its embassy in 1926. After the Spanish Civil War, it was refurbished with fine furnishings, including crystal chandeliers from Spain and priceless eighteenth-century tapestries woven for the Royal Palace in Madrid. (The Sixteenth Street house is now slated to become a Spanish cultural center when the ambassador moves to a new Foxhall Road residence designed by Spanish architect Rafael Moneo.)

In 1921, Mexico had purchased a buff brick mansion a block away, later customizing it with intricate Mexican tile work, including a mural depicting the country's two great volcanoes. Mexican artist Roberto Cueva del Rio spent seven years painting colorful murals that cover the walls around the central staircase and highlight events in Mexican history. In 1923, the Italian ambassador, a trained architect himself, worked with New York architects Warren and Wetmore to recreate a Renaissance palazzo almost directly across the street. Filled with art treasures from Italy, the house was perfectly suited to its purpose. It remained both chancery and official residence until 1976, when the ambassador moved to a Tudor-style villa adjacent to Rock Creek Park – and already appropriately named Firenze House by its prior owners. More recently, the Italians moved to a splendid new chancery on Massachusetts Avenue designed by Piero Sartogo Architetti of Rome. The former edifice on Sixteenth Street now awaits a new owner and a new use.

By the 1920s, upper Sixteenth Street in the vicinity of the Italian Embassy had become Washington's first Embassy Row. Few additional embassies opted for that locale, however. It was soon eclipsed as the place to be by Massachusetts Avenue – or more precisely, the portion that runs from Scott Circle through Sheridan Circle, across Rock Creek Park,

Above

Back façade of the Peruvian Embassy residence. The polished and burnt stone of the historic Peirce Mill in Rock Creek – which dates back to the 1820s – inspired Charles Tompkins' design of the exterior walls of his mansion. The late-Georgian style recalls the 18th century country houses of southeast Pennsylvania and northern Maryland.

Below

In 1945 the Belgian government bought the house which now serves as its Embassy residence from the original owner, Delphine Dodge, the pianist and automobile heiress, who was the widow of Raymond T. Baker.

Pages 40/41

The atmosphere created by the wood, rice paper, bamboo, pagodas, lanterns and stones of the Korean ambassador's residence contrasts strongly with that found in other ambassadors' residences in Washington, where marble, parquet floors, crystal chandeliers, Louis XVI furnishings, ironwork and Aubusson rugs are the rule.

and out to the U.S. Naval Observatory. (The observatory had been established on a hilltop surrounded by seventy-three acres of open land in the 1890s.) That stretch of Massachusetts Avenue is now called Embassy Row, and more than half of the residences illustrated in this volume are located in that vicinity.

At the close of the "Roaring Twenties," fortunes shrank with the onset of the Depression. No longer able to pay for scores of servants or maintain an opulent lifestyle, the owners of many of Washington's great houses sought buyers, but few private individuals could afford such dwellings. Just when the houses might have been subdivided into flats or even demolished in favor of large apartment blocks, new buyers appeared – foreign governments looking for expanded residential and office quarters with prime locations. They began buying up "pre-owned" villas around Sheridan Circle and Kalorama.

The serendipitous intervention of foreign diplomats was what spared Washington's treasure trove of historic houses from near certain destruction. What the city lost in terms of tax revenues (embassies are exempt from D.C. property taxes), it recouped in numerous other ways when the houses were purchased and converted into embassies. Turkey purchased the Everett House in 1933, for example, Greece purchased the Jennings House in

The Government of Brazil bought the mansion which now serves as its embassy residence in 1934. It is the work of John Russell Pope, who was also the architect of the Jefferson Memorial, the original National Gallery and Meridian House.

Above, left

The mansion which has housed the Austrian Ambassador's residence since 1958 has a four-column portico, a Mediterranean-style façade in white stucco and green tiles. The architect Appleton Clark, Jr. designed it in 1925.

Above, right

Front view of the residence of the Ambassador of South Africa. Situated in the tranquil setting of exclusive Embassy Row, it was constructed in 1935 to replace the house that South Africa had rented for the residence and chancery of its legation for many years. In 1964, the offices were moved to a building that was erected next door. The façade alone merits the interest of the passerby, for the Cape Dutch style which inspired it.

1937, Colombia purchased the Gaff House in 1944, and Indonesia purchased the Walsh-McLean House (for a fraction of its original cost) in 1951.

Because many of these houses were acquired fully furnished and because they featured one-of-a-kind interiors, each embassy faced the dilemma of how to maintain the integrity of the original décor while customizing the interiors to showcase its own national identity. As the photographs here show, individual embassies have achieved a remarkable synthesis, interweaving traditions to enhance the look of their public rooms. Overall, their success underscores the power of cultural fusion.

The historic Gaff House, now the residence of the Colombian ambassador, illustrates this well. Although just a block from Dupont Circle, the house is a quiet refuge from the bustle of the surrounding city. For the exterior, architect de Sibour chose red brick contrasted by buff-colored limestone quoins that accentuate the corners, windows, and the six chimneystacks. He created an inviting entrance sequence that takes visitors from a raised vestibule overlooking an enclosed courtyard, through marvelous iron and glass doors to an entrance hall, and on to a reception hall. The reception hall features oak-paneled walls, a richly carved staircase that leads to the ambassador's private quarters on the second floor, a welcoming fireplace, huge north-facing windows, and a bronze baroque chandelier. A spacious drawing room faces east to catch the morning light, and it is connected by a hall to an equally impressive dining room facing north. The mirrored ballroom, featured on the cover of this volume, faces west to capture the evening light. The two-storied ballroom, with its elliptical skylight, its graceful arches articulated by intricately-detailed white plaster trim, and

Opposite page
*The architectural features
of the Colombian Embassy
residence have been described
by the experts as an example
of "coordinated eclecticism".
It was modeled on the
Château Balleroy: only the
moat and balustrades are
missing. This mansion is one
of the bastions of the Dupont
Circle historic circuit.*

Above, left
*The present residence
of the Icelandic Embassy,
located in the Kalorama
neighborhood, was the
temporary center of activities
of Madame Chiang Kai-shek
when she visited Washington.
She was considered the direct
envoy of her husband before
the government of the United
States, despite her lack of an
official portfolio or title.*

Above, right
*This mansion that serves as
the Embassy residence of
Portugal was purchased by
its government in 1946. The
architect Frederick Brooks
oversaw the expansion and
renovation; but not the
interior design. Leonardo
Castro Freire took charge of
the décor. The country's shield
presides over the entrance.*

its curved orchestra balcony wrapped in a white filigree of cast iron, would surely be treasured by any connoisseur of architectural or social history.

Like so many others, the Colombians faced the challenge (and expense) of maintaining
the historic house's tradition while also somehow giving it a Colombian personality. But
how? First, they removed drywall that concealed an exquisitely crafted Tudor-style ceiling
and restored the ceiling. They removed wall-to-wall carpeting and restored the fine oak
floors. On the exterior, they set about the task of properly restoring the lustre to the
imported bricks. Then, to the mix of original furnishings, including antique clocks and
Louis XVI chairs, they added an exuberant collection of modern art that represents their
own culture – art lent by and purchased from Colombian and other Latin American artists.
There is abstract sculpture and painting, but much of the art is distinctly Colombian in
content. For example, framed drawings by Colombian artist Ana Mercedes Hoyos complement the restrained décor of the drawing room and larger and bolder paintings by the
same artist add flair to other rooms. With its sensuous line work and vibrant colors, Hoyos'
work celebrates the landscape and culture of Colombia's San Basilio de Palenque and its
Afro-Colombian heritage. Bouquets of fresh Colombian roses add festive color and scent
to all of the rooms.

Some ambassadors bring their own art collections with them, but most of the residences have art of their own – art that has been purchased, donated, or loaned. In the
newest residences, art and furniture are commissioned for specific spaces and the artists
and craftsmen are almost always from the countries themselves. In this way, the resi-

dences provide an audience for work that deserves international attention. For precisely the same reasons, American embassy residences exhibit the work of American artists and craftsmen. Some art is donated, but U.S. ambassadors are able to make their own selections and borrow art from the nation's leading museums and galleries for that purpose.

While foreign governments were acquiring historic houses in Washington, the United States also purchased a sizable number of historic houses, restored them with care, and turned them into prized American embassy properties overseas. Prague's Schoenborn Palace (acquired in 1925) and Rome's Palazzo Margherita (acquired in 1945) were among the most distinguished houses purchased for use as chanceries. American heiress Barbara Hutton gave her London residence, Winfield House, to the State Department as a residence for the American ambassador just after World War II. Taking advantage of a severely depressed postwar real estate market, the Department was also able to buy a majestic Paris mansion originally built in 1855 for the Baroness de Pontalba and subsequently owned and enlarged by the Baron Edmond de Rothschild. Both residences continue to accommodate U.S. ambassadors in style.

Back of the ambassadorial residence of the European Commission, in the exclusive Kalorama neighborhood of Washington. The house was built in 1922-23 and designed by William Bottomley, one of the most prestigious architects of the era, who chose the Classical Revival style for the design. The European Commission acquired it for its ambassadors in 1970. Previous occupants included C. Douglas Dillon, Under Secretary of State in the Eisenhower administration and Secretary of the Treasury under President Kennedy.

The U.S. government did not build its own embassies overseas until there was widespread feeling in Washington that the United States was suffering in comparison to the other world powers. That was not until the late 1920s. One building that caught the eye of members of Congress was the new British embassy on Massachusetts Avenue designed by renowned British architect Sir Edwin Lutyens and completed in 1931 – about the time that other countries were beginning to convert nearby mansions to embassy use. The British example not only sparked American interest in embassy architecture but also served as a magnet that drew other foreign missions to locate nearby in the vicinity of the Observatory. Lutyens designed it in the style of a country house, incorporating elements associated with American colonial and English Arts and Crafts architecture. With lions guarding its gates and an expansive terrace opening onto picturesque gardens, the red brick building set a new standard for stateliness in embassy design. Moreover, it was quintessentially British from the ground up.

Also in 1931, the Norwegian ambassador and his staff moved into a new embassy designed for them just across from the entrance to the Observatory grounds (which now

The Moroccan government bought this house in Bethesda, Maryland in 1998 for its Embassy residence, to replace the former one in downtown Washington. The developer Michael Nash built this mansion on Clewerwall Drive in 1979.

also include the residence of the U.S. Vice-President). For Norway, and similarly for South Africa, John J. Whelan designed houses with the fine proportions and classical detailing associated with English Georgian architecture. Nearby, for diplomats from the Vatican, Frederick V. Murphy designed a legation modeled on Roman tradition. Completed in 1939, the spare, symmetrical, limestone-clad building was widely admired – so much so that when the U.S. State Department was beset by criticism of its postwar embassies in 1953, it admonished its chief architect to abandon avant-garde modernist architecture and use the Vatican's building as a model for all future U.S. embassies. (He bravely refused, but that is another story entirely.)

As the United States grew in stature as a world power, diplomatic delegations to Washington increased steadily in size and rank. Many required additional room for expanded operations. This led to the gradual separation of residences from offices and a scramble for new space, particularly office space. By the early 1960s, there were close to 100 foreign missions in the U.S. capital and the number climbed as nations won independence in Africa and elsewhere.

Since the British set the standard, other nations have followed with "signature" chanceries specifically designed to establish political presence and emphasize national identity. Germany retained German architect Egon Eiermann to design a chancery near Foxhall Road in 1964. In a bold move and a break with tradition, Canada consolidated its embassy offices in 1989 and moved far from other chanceries to a site on Pennsylvania Avenue at the foot of Capitol Hill. Canadian architect Arthur Erickson designed the Canadian chancery that, through its location and its architecture, calls attention to the

The elegant gray stone mansion at Sheridan Circle and 23rd street, N.W., has long been the residence of the Ambassador of Turkey. The architecture is a fusion of design elements spanning three centuries. The striking façade – with its fluted columns, paneled balustrades, and elaborate portico – appears to have been made to order for its long-term residents – the nation recognized as the bridge between Europe and Asia.

uniqueness of the relationship between Canada and its host. And both Finland and Italy moved from relatively inaccessible locations and cramped quarters to larger and far more prominent sites on Massachusetts Avenue. The Finns moved into a exquisitely-crafted glass box designed by Finnish architects Heikkinen and Komonen (1994), and the Italians established themselves in a striking new chancery designed for them by Italian architect Sartogo (2000), who took his inspiration, in part, from L'Enfant's plan for Washington. Both countries significantly raised their public profile in the capital with these new office structures.

But historically, these were exceptions because embassy efforts to relocate or expand had been running into local opposition for many years as D.C. neighbors blocked proposed plans for new construction. They objected to the loss of parking spaces and the intrusion of business operations into areas zoned for residential use. As a result of public outcry in the early 1960s, Congress had called on the State Department to clamp down on the expansion of foreign missions in established neighborhoods. This curtailed available options.

Recognizing the absence of affordable building sites in the parts of town where chanceries wanted to congregate, the State Department worked with D.C. and federal officials to plan an enclave for new chanceries on thirty-four acres of federal property in Northwest, D.C. Created in 1968 and located at the intersection of Connecticut Avenue and Van Ness Street, the International Chancery Center provided building sites on which fifteen countries (Austria, Bahrain, Bangladesh, Brunei, Egypt, Ethiopia, Ghana, Israel, Jordan, Kuwait, Malaysia, Nigeria, Singapore, Slovakia, and the United Arab Emirates) have constructed office buildings since the early 1980s. Most of them incorporate themes as-

Opposite page
The red brick Georgian-style Canadian Embassy residence, with vistas of Rock Creek Park, was purchased by the Canadian government in 1947. The architect, Nathan Wyeth, also designed the embassies of Russia and Chile, the Mexican Cultural Institute and the Key and Tidal Basin bridges.

Above, left
In 1960 the Government of Guatemala purchased this welcoming mansion built in 1919. Even though it is not in the middle of the jungle, like the magnificent Mayan archeological site of Tikal, it does enjoy the abundant green space of neighboring Rock Creek Park.

Above, right
Built on top of a small hill, the Panamanian Embassy residence abuts the chancery. In fact, when the residence was acquired in 1942, the offices and the residence functioned together. A year later, another building, in the same style as the residence, was erected to house the offices.

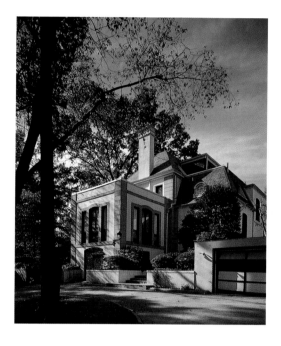 

sociated with each country's architectural heritage (although most were designed by American architects). Pakistan's chancery is under construction. Once China and Morocco proceed with their plans, the center will be full. Already the search is on for more sites. Planners are weighing the costs and benefits of locating chanceries near one another and requiring them to locate within the District of Columbia, and they are trying to identify new options for facilities that increasingly require more space and more security.

Embassy residences are another matter. First of all, unlike chanceries they co-exist comfortably with neighbors in many parts of town, including Spring Valley, Chevy Chase, and along Foxhall Road. Secondly, they are permitted to locate outside of the District of Columbia. Some have moved to suburban locations in Maryland and Virginia, attracted by low costs, good schools, privacy, and other factors. Since many chanceries have assumed representational functions once performed by residences, it is less important for the residences to be prominently located. Not everyone, however, has chosen to retreat from visibility.

Just as there are "signature" chanceries, there are "signature" residences, and they are among Washington's premier modern landmarks. Most have been designed by noted architects from each country as a way of underscoring the cultural importance of such commissions. Denmark was the first to build a modern embassy (both residence and chancery). In the early 1960s, when Lauritzen created the modernist jewel for Denmark, there was absolutely nothing like it in town and it focused widespread attention on Denmark and its role as a leading source for design innovation. Set on a secluded site overlooking Rock Creek Park, the embassy features large expanses of glass and white marble walls, floors, and stairs. The residence is connected to the chancery by a glass corridor, but both retain their autonomy – the chancery as a workplace and the residence as a home. The combination of traditional pieces with Danish modern furnishings – including Lauritzen's glittering chandeliers and Verner Panlon's lamps that pay homage to designs by Arne Jacobsen, Denmark's leading modernist – adds warmth to the cool functionalist aesthetic.

Faced with the need to expand its Massachusetts Avenue facility in the 1970s, Japan turned to Japanese architect Masao Kinoshita and relocated its ambassador's residence to a spacious modern villa that showcases Japanese art and tradition. Similarly, Korea hired architect Swoo-Guen Kim, who conveyed a distinctly Korean sensibility in his design for the official residence for the Korean ambassador. Kim took his cue from Korean vernacular tradition and incorporated such details as rice-paper screens and stone lanterns into the house and its gardens (1986).

Of all the new residences, none has caused more sensation than O.M. Ungers' 1988 house for the German ambassador. On a sharply-angled site high above Foxhall Road, it makes a dramatic statement about classicism expressed in a formal modernist idiom. Designed as a total work of art, the residence is a showplace for contemporary German art and furnishings and an impressive setting for entertainment. Its public rooms are arranged on an axial plan on either side of a soaring central hall that runs the length of the residence and leads to a breathtaking view of the city at night. The art by German artists was selected by the architect to complement the post-modern architecture. Some was designed purposely for the gridded spaces. Like all of the other high-profile residences, this one somehow also manages to accommodate the ambassador and his family. Here, as elsewhere, the family quarters are off-limits to visitors.

New buildings are costly, and not every nation can afford to build its own residence or office, but in the arena of public diplomacy where images convey information, architecture can often convey a message more effectively than any public relations program. As pictured in this volume, embassies are buildings that convincingly convey prosperity and dependability. They read as billboards that proclaim shared civic values. The message may be subtle (and even misleading), but diplomacy is a subtle art. Buildings in serious disrepair convey an opposite message, generally a suggestion of political or economic instability. Dilapidated buildings and an abandoned construction site on Massachusetts Avenue, once envisioned as a new embassy for The Ivory Coast, now stand as a poignant reminder of the turmoil in that West African nation.

The number of embassies in Washington increased sharply after the demise of the Soviet Union and is likely to increase further. The current total of 175 could easily grow if political fragmentation continues to spawn new nation-states. As settings for entertainment and exchange, the embassy houses in this volume play a vital role in the life of the capital and serve as indispensable catalysts for diplomatic discourse.

Located at number 2221 Kalorama Avenue, the current French Embassy was built in 1910 by Jules Henri de Sibour (the same architect that designed the Colombian Embassy) for the millionaire William D. Lawrence. There is no clear agreement on the façade's style. For some, it is Neo-Tudor, for others Norman, Vanderbilt or Jacobean. It has been the property of the French government since 1936.

Pages 56/57
In the design of this residence that houses the Venezuelan Embassy one can see the influence of Frank Lloyd Wright. Chester A. Patterson, the architect of this mansion, was his disciple.

ARGENTINA

Clark Waggeman went to the Law School of The Catholic University of America in Washington, at the request of his father. He spoke four languages but never formally studied architecture, which was not an impediment for him to begin designing residences – in abundance. The first one was on Connecticut Avenue; the last one was for himself, his dream house, and number one hundred of his career. He died suddenly in 1919 – at 42 – during the influenza epidemic that devastated the city.

The mansion located at 1600 New Hampshire Avenue – one of the many built by Waggeman – is currently the Argentine chancery. The caption of a photograph published by the Washington Post on the 14th of May 1950 described it as "…a home of considerable proportions for a single gentleman…The rooms have high ceilings which are suitable for social evenings, especially for the large and popular buffet-dinners," (alluding perhaps to the typical roasts and mixed grills).

What the press note did not say was that the home had been purchased by the Government of Argentina for $ 300 000 in 1913 during the period when its official representative before the United States was Minister Rómulo Naon, the former Minister of Justice of President José Figueroa Alcorta. The house was destined, at the beginning, for the residence of the ambassadors. In 1947 Argentina bought a second property (for a third of the cost of the first), on Q Street, which was briefly used as the chancery. Then a practical barter definitively inverted the functions of both buildings. The buildings are so close, as siblings and neighbors, that they end up being confused with one another.

In fact, it is a complete certainty that Waggeman also designed the current residence of the Ambassador of Argentina in 1914. The house, located in the popular Dupont Circle area, is both elegant and functional. It has, of course, some interesting innovations, such as the great dining hall, located on the second floor, with its spectacular Sheraton-style table. The magnificent paintings by the prolific Buenos Aires painter and architect Miguel Ocampo hang on three of the four walls of the room. According to the artist's own confession, he began to paint at age seven, simply because he liked to. "I lived in the country, very close to horses and rural work. There I found my inspiration", he recalled in an interview. Today, at age 80, – he was in the Foreign Service for years – he is an artist of indisputable international stature.

Between the dining room and the drawing room, the music room beckons the guest to linger. An intimate *fin-de-siècle* atmosphere is created by the golden appliqués, the small lamps set on bombé-style chests, the Louis XVI-style chairs and the piano. On the first floor is the library, a room of elegant intimacy. It welcomes one with its armchairs upholstered in raw linen. The "asados" – Argentinean-style cookouts – take place outside in the garden. They are the typical Argentine culinary and social ritual and only require as a pretext the pleasure of getting together around the grill.

The Oval Salon serves as a ballroom and a site for the frequent receptions and is often the preferred space when Argentinean artists perform in town. A wide band of 24 karat gold, with floral motifs and coats of arms that bear the letters "R. A." (Argentine Republic), lines the ceiling of the ballroom. Under the ceiling, a cornice hides 450 small lights! Nothing is left in the dark, least of all the valuable collection of paintings by outstanding national artists, such as Casal, Capurro, Loza, Homero, Colombres and Russo.

Above
Situated between the dining room and the salon, the music room invites the guest to linger. An intimate fin-de-siècle atmosphere is created by the golden appliqués, the small lamps set on bombé-style chests and the Louis XVI-style chairs: the piano completes the illusion.

Below
The library, located on the first floor, is an elegantly intimate room, with its comfortable armchairs upholstered in raw linen.

Opposite page
The music room, located on the second floor. In the background, an imposing candelabrum illuminates one of the paintings by the artist Miguel Ocampo in the dining room.

One of the special things
about this residence is
the location of the dining
room on the second floor.
The Sheraton table can
seat up to 22 for formal
dinners. A collection of
paintings by the celebrated
Buenos Aires artist and
architect Miguel Ocampo,
specially commissioned for
the residence, hangs in
this room.

AUSTRIA

If you use your imagination while crossing the threshold of this residence you'll feel yourself approaching a splendorous era, full of powerful dynasties, of emperors and empresses who knew the taste of conquest and of utter ruin.

Appleton P. Clark, Jr., who in his sixty-year career devoted himself to many diverse projects, was one of the most prominent and prolific architects of the early 20th century, and he designed the house in 1925. The Austrian government didn't actually buy it until much later, in 1958, but unlike other diplomatic missions, this one hasn't needed expansion or renovation. With the exception of an attic built ten years ago, the house remains as it was at its conception. The Mediterranean style is still on display, with white stucco and green tiles, and the four solid columns on the portico. When you step into the ample vestibule with its black and white marble floors, you cannot help thinking that this would be the ideal dance floor for a good waltz.

In each room of the residence, history and art join hands. On a wall in the entrance, a famous painting of the Schönbrunn Palace, in Vienna, welcomes the visitor. And as one would expect, Biedermeier-style furniture, very much in vogue in Central and Northern Europe, especially in Austria and Germany during the 19th century, appears throughout the three floors. These days, recognizing them isn't as easy as one might think. Experts in the Biedermeier style warn that one of the most common mistakes people make is to assume that any furniture of light wood, bordered in black, is a Biedermeier. Given the great variety of woods used, they explain, it becomes impossible to recognize a Biedermeier solely by color or contrast, so the details and forms that characterize them must be studied as well. But that's another story entirely.

In the principal salon, the rule of the Austro-Hungarian Empire announces itself in the heavy glass candelabra, the Boesendorfer grand piano, the fine 18th century furniture and the enigmatic smile of the princess Anna Maria, depicted in a portrait. And while we're on the subject of dynasties, there is another one present, that of Emperor Franz I of Austria, who resigned in 1804 as Franz II of Germany, when most of the German princes allied themselves with Napoleon. Franz I had to marry his daughter off to Napoleon. He, nevertheless, continued to fight Napoleon and presided over the Congress of Vienna in 1815, when the five monarchs of England, Russia, Prussia, Austria and France negotiated the peace treaty after the Napoleonic wars.

Close in distance and in ideals, is the portrait of his political counselor and Chancellor, Prince Klemens von Metternich, a work of the school of Sir Thomas Lawrence. The government asked that the painting be returned to Vienna, but the answer was a categorical *nein*.

Fine objects abound but there is no excess or squander in the decoration. Each detail is precise; everything is in its place. Over the marble fireplace, an imposing Baroque mirror reflects the silhouettes of a 19th century French clock and two porcelain figures of the Lippizzaner horses, with riders, of the Spanish Equestrian School of Vienna. A pair of Persian rugs covers the parquet floor. Elizabeth Moser, the spouse of the Ambassador

Art and history join hands. Fine 18th century furniture displayed without excess. In the back, the portrait of Emperor Franz I of Austria, who had to marry his daughter off to Napoleon. There is also a portrait of Chancellor Metternich by a student of Sir Thomas Lawrence. The Austro-Hungarian Empire is present.

and daughter of a collector, is an expert on rugs. She explains that a rug's origins are recognized by the motifs and colors used, and the quality shows in the knots. "The tighter the knot, the finer the rug," she says. In the kitchen, she opens an armoire and shows off her china enthusiastically. One by one, the Lobmeier crystal glasses appear, along with the Riedel ones, followed by the famous Ausgarten porcelain: they have been made by dexterous artisans for over two centuries and are rarely found outside Austria itself. The government makes the china available to its embassies abroad. Thus, no matter where in the world you are, when dinner is served, Austria sets the table.

Left
*An ample marble hall,
which resounds with
waltzes, leads to the rooms
on the second floor.*

Above
*View of the area next to the
staircase leading up to the
third floor. On the wall hangs
a Gobelin depicting a typical
Austrian landscape. A heavy
Viennese crystal chandelier
illuminates the room.*

69

BELGIUM

Someone once said that no one really knows for whom they ultimately work and it is particularly opportune in the case of the residence of the Belgian ambassadors. How could the Marquis of Rothelin imagine that the small palace that he built for himself in Paris between 1700 and 1704 – the French architect Pierre Lassurance drew up the plans – would be reproduced to the letter in a Washington, D.C. mansion in 1931?

But that was precisely what Raymond Baker, the former director of the Mint in Woodrow Wilson's administration and his wife, the automobile heiress and concert pianist Delphine Dodge, wanted: to have their very own Hôtel de Charolais, as the Marquis' old home is currently known. The difference is in the surroundings. While the original is on the Rue de Grenelle, the replica rests against a dense forest; here, from the back terrace, you can see the winding Potomac and beyond, far beyond, the majestic Blue Ridge Mountains.

When it came time to choose an architect, the Baker Dodges never doubted that it had to be Philadelphia's Horace Trumbauer who, instead of designing the neo-classical homes that were the fashion of the era, distinguished himself by specializing in classical 18th century-style ones. Trumbauer also designed Washington's former Ritz-Carlton Hotel, now the Sheraton International.

When it came to interior decoration the couple were not reticent about their inspiration: the very 18th century Château de Villarceaux on the Ile-de-France. Edouard Hitau, a famous decorator from the House of Lucien Alvoine et Compagnie, was brought from Paris to do the job. He returned in 1935, when Mrs. Baker, now widowed, decided to rent the residence to her former mother-in-law Mrs. Edward T. Stotesbury, then known as one of the empresses of Palm Beach. And Hitau returned yet again in 1945, at the request of the first Belgian ambassador to inhabit the property, soon after his country purchased the mansion for the residence of its representatives in the nation's capital.

But the reproductions and duplications do not end here. The library is a faithful replica of the George Hoentschel Library, which was donated by J. Pierpont Morgan to the Metropolitan Museum of Art in New York in 1908. Nevertheless this fondness for copying, which could have produced a terrifying aesthetic result, came out beautifully in the end. And, in fact, when the capital's residents talk about the embassies worth seeing, Belgium's house is never missing from the list. It has been described as harmonious, private, aristocratic, warm and romantic. Every adjective is fitting. And they fit so well that, when the time comes to think about idyllic scenarios for the myriad grand events celebrated in this metropolis to benefit social and cultural institutions, the Belgian government is often asked to lend its lovely setting. Indeed, the forty-fourth Opera Ball, one of the social milestones of the city, was held in this residence in 2002. Betty Scripps Harvey, one of the star hostesses of the capital, presided over the event. The Ambassador of Belgium at the time, Alex Reyn, and his spouse Rita, joined Mrs. Harvey and the tenor Plácido Domingo, the artistic director of the Washington Opera, in greeting the

If there is something truly original about this mansion, it is that it never aspired to be original. From its conception in 1931, the idea was to build the best possible replica of the Hôtel de Maître in Paris which was designed by the French architect Pierre Lassurance. It was built on the Rue de Grenelle for the Marquis of Rothelin and is known today as the Hôtel de Charolais.

The Baker Dodge couple were fanatic Francophiles and never reticent about their inspiration and model in interior decoration: the 18th century Château de Villarceau on the Île-de-France. The interior designer Edouard Hitau, of the house of Lucien Alvoine et Compagnie, was brought from Paris to decorate the principal salons. It is thought that the current décor remains faithful, in large part, to the 1931 original. The paintings by contemporary Belgian artists that hang on the walls of this grand salon are part of the personal collection of Ambassador and Madame Reyn. A large antique Louis XVI Royal Aubusson tapestry covers the floor.

guests as they entered. Apart from the extraordinary amount of money raised, people are still talking with admiration about the imposing two-story tent erected in the back garden that recreated Belgian King Leopold II's greenhouse and, above all, the fragrance that emanated from it.

There was an endless table that paid homage to the national cuisine, especially Belgian chocolate, laden with *gâteaux, mousses, profiteroles, crêpes,* baskets of raspberries and strawberries on chocolate napkins and chocolate trays. All these awaited the 500 guests for dessert. They had previously dined at 22 other embassies, or feasted at what are called pre-ball dinners in Washington diplomatic *argot*. This time, Belgium was in charge of the dancing, the calories and the making of an unforgettable evening.

The room is a faithful replica of the George Hoentschel Library, donated by J. Pierpont Morgan to the Metropolitan Museum of Art in New York in 1908. Its paneled walls in natural-finish oak are a fine example of the Regency style of decoration.

A pair of 18th century paintings of ruins, a subject popular in England and France in that era, are displayed on the walls of the dining room. Two 18th century French terracotta figures are set in shell niches. The large Regency table is laid with Belgian linen and Val St. Lambert crystal.

BOLIVIA

This lovely home was built at the beginning of the last century. It was then known as the "White Mansion" after its first owner, Senator White, but it could also have been because of the color of the façade. In 1941 it became the property of the Bolivian government. One of the reasons for the purchase was the house's Spanish Colonial style, so prevalent in various cities in Bolivia. Another is its great beauty, which makes the residence stand out in the neighborhood, and its privileged location on Embassy Row among the residences and chanceries of Brazil and Great Britain.

From the time it was acquired, in the era of Ambassador Fernando Guachalla, to the present, over 22 diplomats have resided there and there have been many renovations and much remodeling, but its original architectural style has always been preserved and its art collections have always grown. In these collections, seen a few steps from the entrance, centuries of Bolivian history are summarized.

The Pre-Columbian ceramics on the entrance hall console immediately remind us of the historical significance of the indigenous population in the culture and traditions of the nation. Currently the native peoples, mostly Quechuas and Aymaras, make up 52% of the population of the country. And even though Spanish is the official language of Bolivia, Quechua, Aymara and Guaraní are spoken throughout the country.

The spectacular silverware in the dining room, especially a mirror with an antique, hand-carved Potosí silver frame, leads one to reflect on the perfection achieved by the people who worked with that metal. Many centuries before gold fever put California on the map for thousands of adventurers, Potosí, a state in the southwest of Bolivia, had been the site of a similar phenomenon: a silver rush.

The discovery of the first vein is attributed to Diego Huallpa, an indigenous inhabitant of the area. When and how remain matters of doubt. It is said that it took place way back in 1545, when he climbed the "majestic mountain", *Sumaj Orcko*, in search of some lost llamas and, in the midst of wild grassland, found the millionaire vein of native silver. There is yet another version, always with Huallpa in the starring role and *Sumaj Orcko* as the setting. It tells that when Huallpa, freezing on the high slopes, lit a fire to warm himself, the mineral started to melt and appeared as threads of the purest silver. The Spanish, who had already arrived in Bolivia, heard the story and left their homes to pursue the dream of making a fortune in America.

It was not easy to make the mountain yield up its riches. Access to it was extremely difficult and the altitude, the cold and the desolateness of the zone all created very harsh working conditions. Nevertheless, the amount extracted was so great that Emperor Carlos V granted Potosí the title of "Imperial City" and the term "it is worth a Potosí" was coined.

There were highs and lows in the silver boom, which continued until the middle of the 19th century, when tin, silver's poor relation till then, grew in importance with the fall of silver prices and the expansion of industries (like automotive and food products)

The main drawing room is furnished with Victorian pieces purchased by Simón Patiño, the Bolivian tin magnate and one of the richest men in the world of his time. The silk carpet is a hand-woven Persian one that is more than a 100 years old. The painting is an original by the Irish artist G. O'Connor, titled Dama Antigua.

Page 78, left
The Pre-Columbian ceramics on the entrance hall console immediately remind us of the historical significance of the indigenous peoples in the culture and traditions of the country. The work depicting two natives figures is by Gil Imana.

Page 78, right
Silver goblets engraved with the Bolivian seal are exhibited on a built-in shelf on the wall of the main dining room.

which needed tin as a raw material. Bolivia became the biggest producer of tin in the world.

History is never far from view in Potosí, where the old mines were adapted to the exploitation of tin. This takes us to another part of the embassy: the main drawing room, furnished with Victorian pieces purchased by the Bolivian magnate, Simón Patiño, who with talent, hard work and vision became the King of Tin and the richest man in South America.

Opposite page
The Embassy's collection of Bolivian art includes oil paintings, water colors, statues and lithographs by some of the most respected artists of Bolivia.

BRAZIL

As soon as Ambassador Oswaldo Aranha learned, in 1934, that McCormick House was for sale, he decided that it was time to put an end to the peregrinations of Brazil's representatives. President James Monroe recognized Brazil's independence in 1824, and Ambassador Aranha felt it was high time that Brazil had its own ambassador's residence, fit for the representative of the government of the United States of Brazil. The moment had come to stop the renting of houses and furnishings.

Once the deal was closed, they bought the land next to the mansion, and that same year they started to build the Chancery. The Chancery was later demolished to make room, in 1971, for a magnificent three-story crystal cube, supported by concrete pillars, that speaks volumes about the beauty and excellence of contemporary Brazilian architecture. The contrast between these sibling, neighboring structures is astonishing, even though the lawns and gardens ably fulfill their harmonizing tasks. To understand their differences, one must go back to their conception.

It was not the government of Brazil which decided that its ambassadors' residence would rise on the Pretty Prospect triangle; it only decided where the Chancery would go. The first owner and lady of the house selected the mansion's location. Katherine Medill McCormick was a rich heiress – articulate, intelligent, trilingual – and the indefatigable companion of Robert Sanderson McCormick. Her husband, a career diplomat, was the U.S. Ambassador in Paris, Rome, Vienna and Saint Petersburg. When the time came to settle down permanently, they opted to build in Washington, and right on Massachusetts Avenue, in an era when no one imagined that the avenue would become the new Embassy Row. This was a none too conventional decision, because at that time it was a bit far from downtown. The choice of John Russell Pope as the mansion's architect was a much more conventional move. Pope was considered one of the best house designers in the United States. He would later enter the history books as the architect of the National Gallery's West Wing, the Jefferson Memorial and the National Archives, all architectural milestones in the U.S. capital. Later, but only much later, would he be criticized to death by the modernists, who raised the cry, "Enough of Pope's Parthenons!" If consistency with his aesthetic ideals throughout his life was for some his great mistake, others think that it is an important aspect of his legacy.

In fact, he was famous and envied for his ability to reconcile the demands, wishes and whims of his clients with his personal style. And "personal" means just that. The critics of his work never used the word "imitator." He was a fanatical admirer of classical antiquity and his visits to Italy and Greece only confirmed his conviction that he was in the right. He conceived his projects within the classical framework and never compromised his style. According to his aesthetic codes, beauty should simply be… splendid and grand. Column galleries and magnificent staircases balanced the severity of his façades. His formula, if it can be defined, was one of rich interiors and austere exteriors. The ex-McCormick house is a very good example of his signature style. The original owners designed the mansion with its twenty-five rooms to house the great variety and quantity of furniture, rugs, tapestries and

White and brown are the dominant colors in the dining room; they echo the Victorian Portuguese furnishings as well as the 17th century English-style ceiling.

This was originally the magnificent McCormick library. It is now a salon on the first floor near the stairs. The 19th century paper mural describing scenes of colonial Brazil, by the famous Bavarian artist Johann Moritz Rugendas, is the centerpiece of this room.

objets they had collected in the course of their frequent travels. Many of the furnishings were later acquired, along with the mansion, by the government of Brazil.

Today, what they initially purchased, along with the additions made over the years and the personal effects donated by successive ambassadorial families, come together to form a magic union of light, color and art. This confluence of architecture and décor makes this residence one of the more beautiful and original in the city.

The problem is where to focus one's attention. On the first floor, many opt for the modern sculptures in the vestibule. Others prefer the embassy's painting collection, which includes works by such well-known artists as Portinari, Di Cavalcanti and Eliseu Visconti. But the great majority are fascinated by the 19th century paper mural on the walls of what used to be the library. The mural shows scenes of colonial Brazil, based on drawings made by the Bavarian painter Johann Moritz Rugendas during his visit to the country as a member of the cultural mission sent by Alexander I, the Russian czar. The originals were kept in the Saint Petersburg Museum, and these were used by the French artist Jean Julien Deltil between 1829-30 to manufacture the paper in Jean Zuber & Company's factory in Alsatia. The paper was reprinted various times in the nineteenth and twentieth centuries. Examples of the paper can also be found in the Palace of Itamarati in Río de Janeiro and in a number of private houses in the Brazilian capital.

On the second floor, the very pleasant great salon contrasts with the dramatic dining room ceiling, where the sure and knowing hand of Maria Ignes, the spouse of the current Ambassador Rubens Barbosa, did not hesitate to paint, in dark colors, the irregular geometric panels that decorate the room. And Mme. Barbosa's simple, ethereal and infinite floral arrangements are unforgettable.

Left
A relief by Emanoel Araujo, a lettino by Mies Van der Rohe and sculptures by Kratina, Kenneth Martin and Leslie Smith greet visitors as they come in the entrance hall.

Above
On the Brazilian colonial "arcaz", a jacaranda-wood chest of drawers brought from a church in Paracatu, are the modern sculptures from Ambassador Ruben Barbosa's private collection.

This salon is bigger than
the old library and decorated
very differently. The ceiling
and walls are richly adorned
with Regency-style stucco.
In the ballroom two sitting
areas divide the space. The
floral arrangements reflected
on the mirrors immediately
attract the eye.

CANADA

Elizabeth Maguire, writing at the end of the forties in The Washington Post, was among the first writers to draw attention to the residence of the Ambassador of Canada to the United States. The article praised the red brick Georgian-style house on Rock Creek Park, with its white Ionic columns at the entrance, ample spaces, high ceilings and impressive staircase.

Over half a century later, the mansion is still outstanding, with the same façade, and only a few alterations to its interior. The architect, Nathan Wyeth, who built it in 1931 for John and Katherine Davidge, had trained at the *École des Beaux Arts* in Paris and designed numerous other buildings in Washington during his brilliant career. Among them are the embassies of Russia and Chile and the Mexican Cultural Institute.

He also designed the Key and Tidal Basin bridges, the Battleship Maine Monument at Arlington Cemetery, hospitals, schools, libraries, firehouses and various municipal seats. He was also commissioned to enlarge the West Wing of the White House, including the Oval Office, and the Capitol's Russell Office Building. In his public architecture, Wyeth favored the Colonial and Georgian Revival styles.

The Canadian government purchased the house in 1947. A good part of the furniture, lamps and *objets d'art* in the house came from the Embassy Chancery, located on Massachusetts Avenue, and bought by the government in 1927. According to Maguire's article, the crystal chandelier that hangs in the dining room also made the move from the Chancery.

The residence is a faithful reflection of the welcoming nature of Canada, which shares with the U.S. the longest undefended border in the world and is its largest trading partner. The diversity of Canada, which spans six time zones from east to west, is also reflected in the residence. Summertime, for example, is enjoyed in the sunroom or *loggia*. It has the original quarry tile floor and walls covered with grass cloth.

The furniture is bamboo and glass. In wintertime, the house's occupants prefer to gather around the fireplace in the library. The drawing room is furnished with a piano and antiques from different periods. All the rooms have fireplaces. Hospitality is symbolized by the pineapple, which is carved high on the mahogany doors of the dining and drawing rooms.

The ten provinces and three territories are represented by the works of diverse Canadian artists scattered throughout the residence. Sculptures, drawings, engravings and paintings are found, from the entrance hall to the garden. The sculpture *Mother and Papoose,* by the well-known Inuit artist, Kaka, deserves special mention, as it was part of the Canadian pavilion at Expo'67.

The thick mahogany front doors open onto a foyer and reveal a spectacular circular staircase. The hall's white marble floor, bordered in green marble, has as its center an eleven-point maple leaf, the Canadian symbol for three centuries. An Inuit print, Hunter & Son, *hangs at the bottom of the staircase. It is by Pitalouisa, a celebrated Inuit artist, known for her drawings and prints of the mythical animal and bird figures of her culture.*

Left

The mahogany table, with its original oval shape, was made by the celebrated British furniture designers Arthur Brett & Sons, and seats twenty-four. On the side, the fine gilded mirror complements the marble-covered, Sheridan-style serving table. The carpet is a Karastan. A selection of prints, drawings and sculptures by Inuit artists is proudly displayed. They represent the memory, myths and legends of the Inuit people of the Canadian Arctic.

Above

The doors are mahogany, like those in the dining room. The furnishings include an ebony Steinway piano and antiques from different periods, including two Louis XIV bergères. Facing the fireplace, with its mantel of white marble veined with black, are two Sheridan-style love seats and a pair of Louis XV chairs, upholstered in silk. On the walls of the drawing room hang paintings by Canadian artists David Milne, Christopher Pratt, Maurice Callum and David Blackwood.

CHILE

It took a series of fortuitous events for Chile to come into possession of its present ambassador's residence. John Wyeth had to die in Philadelphia, so that his widow Sarah would move to Washington and buy the land on Massachusetts Avenue. Then Sarah had to conclude that the only person to design it had to be her much sought-after cousin Nathan Wyeth, who was already famous for his buildings and ever-increasing number of honors and awards. In the midst of designing bridges (the Key and Tidal Basin bridges), hospitals (the Emergency and Columbia Hospitals), public buildings (the expansion of the West Wing of the White House, the Oval Office included) and monuments (the Battleship Maine Monument at Arlington Cemetery), he found time to finish a mansion for his relative in 1909 and to go on to build dozens more for prominent residents of the U.S. capital, including the current Russian Ambassador's residence.

Who decided that the exterior of Chile's future home should be Louis XV and that the predominant interior element would be a magnificent double staircase that leads from the first floor to the second? The Wyeth cousins took that secret with them to their graves. It is public knowledge that the internationally-renowned British architect, Sir Edwin Luytens, was inspired by the Wyeth mansion when he built the British Embassy. A group of members of the Luytens Trust recently visited the Chilean Ambassador's residence, making a special trip from England to observe, directly and in living color, the many-angled staircase.

Mrs. Wyeth never knew or heard of all this. She died in 1920 and left her three-story-plus-basement mansion to her son Stuart. He sold it after two years. In June 1923 when the Republic of Chile bought it, it had passed through various hands, the only addition to the house at that time being a brick garage built directly behind it.

Less mysterious, but not altogether clear, is how Chile managed to get together the funds to acquire the house. The oft-repeated story is that their first glimmer of hope appeared on the horizon when one of the negotiators remembered that, when purchasing a World War I ship, Chile had deposited some funds as a guarantee in a U.S. bank. So apart from recovering the funds, someone thought that the bank should be asked to pay a certain amount of interest for having held on to the money for all those years. The bank accepted, and a contract was signed. And thus Beltrán Mathieu, the great Chilean political and diplomatic figure, became the first ambassador to occupy the mansion. Twenty-eight more have followed since his time.

But more unanswered questions remain. When one tries to find out who bought certain pieces of the fine French furnishings in the house, some – like Fernando Balmaceda – maintain that it was during the period of don Félix Nieto who made the purchases with the 120 000 dollars that were donated by the Chilean millionaire Arturo López-Pérez who had found that the residence was "poorly ornamented" during a visit made by the end of 1940.

The residence first underwent serious modifications in 1967, when Ambassador Radomiro Tomic, one of the founders of the Christian Democrats and their 1970 presidential candi-

The magnificent double staircase inspired the internationally-renowned British architect, Sir Edwin Lutyens, when he built the British Embassy. It is considered one of the most spectacular in a city where hundreds vie for the honor. Many were built as central elements in the residences of the first decades of the 20th century.

Entrance hall seen from the staircase. On the left, the Blue Room, where smaller groups of visitors are received. On the right, the principal Drawing Room. Among the many stories of how the Chilean government was able to purchase such a magnificent and well-located mansion, one relates that a Chilean negotiator remembered that Chile had deposited some funds as a guarantee in a U.S. bank when purchasing a World War I ship. So apart from recovering the funds, someone thought that the bank should be asked for some amount in back interest for having held on to the funds for all those years. The bank accepted, and they had the complete sum.

Left

Important paintings by Chilean artists of different schools and periods line the walls of the mansion's three stories: Onofre Jarpa, Pedro Lira, Rafael Correa, Thomas Somerscales, Nemesio Antúnez, José Balmes, Gracia Barrios, Carmen Aldunate, Guillermo Nuñez, Mario Toral, Ricardo Irarrázabal, Francisco De la Puente and Francisco Smythe. The chimney, in the fashion of the era, is the centerpiece of the main drawing room.

date, had a modern salon built next to the dining room. Two doors leading to the new room replaced the two sets of huge windows that surrounded the fireplace. Over the years this room has had many different uses and ambiances. It was a family room, decorated with Chilean furnishings and handicrafts in Tomic's time. Today it has become a multifunctional salon that can seat fifty for a meal or serve as a big reception hall, a concert hall and a site for press conferences. Chilean sculptor Sergio Castillo's beautiful bronze chess set and the striking works of the Chilean painting couple Gracia Barros and José Balmes (on loan to the current Ambassador and Mrs. Andrés Bianchi) shine amidst the austere décor.

Other important changes were introduced by diplomats Felix Nieto, who, because of a cardiac condition, had an elevator built to the second floor, of which not a trace remains, and Walter Muller, who intelligently concluded that a pool would be more important than a garage in Washington's intense hot summers and dove into this work. To José Miguel Barros, an inveterate bibliophile and voracious reader, the residence owes the second floor ambassador's private library, with a desk surrounded by floor-to-ceiling bookcases, which the house lacked until Ambassador Barros solved the problem of what to do with all his books.

In the mid-nineties, Ambassador John Biehl took the bull by the horns and decided to give the nearly century-old mansion the complete renovation it so sorely needed. He modernized the kitchen and reinforced the foundation. Keep in mind that when the mansion was built the traffic on Embassy Row was nowhere as heavy as it is today. Even so, the house still sways with the passing of every heavy truck. Better yet, it trembles. After all, it is Chilean soil…

Opposite page

The residence first underwent serious modifications in 1967 when Ambassador Radomiro Tomic, one of the founders of the Christian Democratic Party and its 1970 presidential candidate, had a modern multipurpose room built next to the dining room. When there are more than 20 diners at the table, the new room is equipped to handle 50.

COLOMBIA

The creative combination of the architect Jules Henri de Sibour and Thomas T. Gaff, the original owner of the house, was a risky one to begin with. The former was born in France, a direct descendant of Louis XVI and the son of a viscount. He came to the United States as a child, and later graduated from Yale and the *École des Beaux Arts* in Paris. The latter hailed from Indiana and was an enormously successful businessman in such diverse fields as distilleries and heavy machinery. Gaff studied at Harvard, Leipzig and Göttingen Universities and was fluent in Latin, French and German. No one expected that the grand house Mr. Gaff wished to build would be a typical Washington residence of the era. Nevertheless, like many mansions of the time that later became embassies, such as the France and Luxembourg residences, it was designed by the prolific Mr. De Sibour, and this meant it would have the requisite magnificent staircase, grand reception salons and colossal chimneys.

When it came to defining the predominant style of the mansion, Gaff specified what he wanted, and de Sibour readily granted it. It has been said that France's Henry IV would immediately recognize the façade's brickwork; that England's Elizabeth I would feel right at home in the dining room; and that when the band struck a waltz, Britain's Edward VII would challenge everyone to take the measure of the dance floor.

In terms of architectural merit, some have affirmed that the residence is a model of "coordinated eclecticism." All that's missing to make it look exactly like the Château Balleroy, the castle that inspired it, is the moat, the arbours and the balustrades.

Criticisms here and there notwithstanding, there is no doubt that this property is considered one of the highlights of the Dupont Circle historical circuit. Gaff wanted to provoke a different impact in each room of the mansion, and he fully achieves this. Each of the three stories in the house is a totally different world, each room a subcontinent.

In 1944, after having rented it for some years, the government of Colombia bought the 1906 mansion. It was owned by Gaff's daughter and chockfull of her personal effects. We explored the house from top to bottom: from the lower depths of the basement to the heights of the attic.

On the basement, we were surprised to find something quite unexpected in the form of the great kitchen. This creates a huge inconvenience: in the winter it becomes almost impossible to ensure that the food stays hot when it reaches the dining room. But we also found something that we had come looking for: a clothes dryer, of Gaff's own invention, a true museum piece that has, in fact, recently been solicited by the Smithsonian.

Halfway between the basement and the first floor is another, much smaller, kitchen-pantry, one of the few renovations of recent years. The other major renovation dates back to 1945, when a small side yard was transformed into the garage.

The large grounds at the back of the house, the real green lung of the original mansion, are now occupied by the Hilton. In the past, the large doors of the ballroom opened onto that garden. But how did it disappear? Rumour has it that an ambassador considered the grounds superfluous and made the decision to sell the land.

The ballroom has been described in various ways. Some call it magnificent, because of its dimensions and others, royal, because of the elaborated plaster-work of its ceilings and walls.

On the first floor our attention is drawn to the dozens of fresh roses – full of the smells and colors of the Savannah of Bogotá – that weekly invade the salons, hallways and dining room of the residence. Works by important Colombian painters line the walls and compete with the oak paneling in the hallways, the stairs, and the sitting and dining rooms.

The sun lights up the principal salons in the morning and in the afternoon floods the ballroom. It is said that it even dances the salsa…

The starring role in the reception hall is taken by the chairs, said to have belonged to the great Victor Hugo. The star of the Elizabethan dining room was an Italian Renaissance armoire brought over from a monastery, but only until the original ceiling was unveiled in all its splendor. The ceiling re-appeared when someone tried to plug a leak and accidentally discovered, under the fake white plaster which had been installed to lighten up the room, a magnificent woodwork ceiling. But the ceiling's woodwork carvings aren't the only magnificent feature. In accordance with Gaff's exquisite, infinitely-detailed plan, the neighboring ballroom's vault reigns alongside the fine woodwork of the dining hall.

This two-story room truly stands apart. It deserves a standing ovation for being unexpected, spacious and very special.

Event Room. This two-story event room was destined to be a multi-use space. It is used as a dining room, a gallery and a concert hall, and also for salsa classes.

It is the scene of some of the most spectacular charity events in the city. The glass doors that surround it used to open onto an opulent garden, before a certain myopic ambassador sold the land. Today a five-star hotel stands on the grounds of the old garden.

This residence was designed to render the visitor speechless. The severity and bareness of the hallway walls stand in frank contrast with the richness and ornateness of the salons that follow.

And no room is a more appropriate reminder of Colombian culture – in which even one's sorrows are danced beautifully. Nevertheless, not everything is music.

The second floor is reserved for the Presidential suite and that of the ambassador's family. It also houses Gaff's library, with some of the original volumes on its shelves. Among others, there is a first edition of "Life on the Mississippi", signed by Mark Twain, and the second volume of the 1884 edition of the works of the English Poet Laureate Alfred Lord Tennyson. On the third floor there is a wing of guest rooms and the servants' quarters.

In the attic, amidst old furniture and mourning doves we found the remnants of the much wept-for elevator. Elevators have incalculable value in houses such as these, where large staircases abound. It was eliminated by an ambassador, with horrendous judgment, and in very good physical condition.

Left
One of the few staircases of its type that has kept the original color of its woodwork, it rises to display a work by Ana Mercedes Hoyos, "Crop Substitution", ("Sustitución de un Cultivo"), more commonly known as "Sunflowers". It is a colorful work that invites you to reflect on one of the most complex problems that afflicts Colombia.

Opposite page
The star of the Elizabethan dining room was an Italian Renaissance armoire, specially brought over from a monastery, until an opportune leak led to the discovery of the original ornamental ceiling. The ceiling had been covered over by a diplomat who found the original a bit lugubrious.

Above and right

The residence is a permanent museum of the best of Colombian art. Some paintings have been loaned by private collectors, others donated by the artists themselves and still others come from the collection of the current Ambassador Luis Alberto Moreno and his wife Gabriela Febres-Cordero de Moreno. Above, a work by Gustavo Zalamea. Opposite, a painting by Ana Mercedes Hoyos.

The chairs that belonged to
Victor Hugo were the stars of
this room until the stunning
Colombian roses outshone
them. Week after week,
Colombian flower exporters
religiously fill the embassy
residence with flowers, to
the barely concealed envy
of other diplomatic missions.

DENMARK

The name of the street suits this diplomatic seat perfectly: "Whitehaven." Maybe "transparent haven" would be even better. But Whitehaven will do.

For white is just what you see upon approaching – to the left, just before the street ends – the resplendent unity made by the residence and chancery of Denmark, posed against the endless trees of Rock Creek Park. A glass corridor unites the two entities; or separates them. Light – a limited resource in northern hemisphere countries – runs rampant in this house. In fact, it cascades into every room. The library might be the sole exception, but the rest of the house is designed as a function of the light.

The entrance hall surprises all who enter because of its distinctiveness. While ornamentation lent magnificence to the old mansions of turn of the century Washington, in the heavy furniture, tapestries and curtains, imposing staircases and embellished ceilings, in this building, constructed in 1958, simplicity reigns. One or two antique pieces appear from time to time on the scene, the kind of furniture with its feet firmly planted on earth, and provide an interesting counterpoint to the grace of the modern pieces, but they are only secondary delights. It is the latter that rule.

It is said that the golden years of Danish design were from 1920 to 1960. Since then the world has learnt from these masters – Denmark and the rest of the Scandinavian countries continue to lead this school of thought – that quality, beauty and function in furnishings are not oxymoronic, nor are they the exclusive patrimony of the privileged classes. Poetry, music and history are not elitist either. Centuries back, Danish educators had made sure that arts and learning were available to all. After this was achieved everyday objects had their turn. This is the Danish way, more an insinuating than an imposing presence. The most perfect example of this was when, on descending the staircase, we looked up and saw, through the dining room door, a chair. It was really much more than a chair; it was the perfect outline of a chair. And therein lie the magic and the difference.

There are also other differences. Here names like Bill, Fred, George and Henry turn into Vilhelm, Frederik, Georg and Henrik.

Henrik Kauffman was the ambassador who in 1947 bought the land where the building sits from the Bliss family, the owners of Dumbarton Oaks. One of the national treasures, Vilhelm Lauritzen, was the chosen architect. The interior décor and the design of some of the furniture – key facts in a country where these are an important source of foreign earnings – are by the world-famous designer Finn Juhl, who worked for ten years in Lauritzen's office.

He had a passion for teak and it is said that this wood owes its apogee to Juhl. He worked the wood like a sculptor and many of his creations are in collections such as the Museum of Modern Art in New York. The dining room table is his work; he designed it jointly with Niels Vodder, the furniture-maker. The candelabra are the work of another famous Dane: the silversmith Georg Jensen. The leather furniture in the library was

Fine design was not an overnight development in Denmark. From the late 18th century onwards one had to pass a written exam to validate one's knowledge in this field. So the great harvest of design in the 20th century was the result of a process that took several centuries. The industry is now one of the country's main sources of foreign earnings. Creativity in the treatment of traditional materials, quality, sophistication and functionality best describe the furnishings of the principal salon of the Danish embassy.

Left

Light is a bit more restricted here, as in any self-respecting library. The ambiance is more intimate and the dark leather furniture contributes to the cozy effect. The furniture is by Borge Mogensen, and the bookshelves by the designer Mogens Kock. Next to the desk, a pair of lounge chairs, each a true work of art of its respective century – the 18th and the 20th – compete for attention.

Above

The author of the luminous entity that is the chancery and the residence was the famous Danish architect Vilhelm Lauritzen. He was also the intellectual author of the constellation of circular lamps in the dining hall, living room and sitting room ceilings. Another notable Dane made them: Louis Poulsen. The dining hall table is by the internationally-known designer Finn Juhl; the china is Royal Copenhagen and all that shines like – and is – silver came from the workshops of the prestigious silversmith Georg Jensen.

Left
Each ambassador contributes his or her own touches. More than a few pieces of furniture and artworks belong to the current ambassadorial couple, Ulrik and Birgitte Federspiel, but most of the furnishings in the property belong to the Danish government. A better showcase would be hard to find.

Opposite page
King Frederik IX and Queen Ingrid inaugurated the embassy on the 12th of October, 1960. Denmark was the first country to daringly adopt a contemporary style for its seat in Washington. From the main entrance hall of the residence – where glass frames Greenland marble – the "elegant simplicity" of the Danes is evident. One or two antique pieces appear on the scene from time to time, the kind of furniture with its feet firmly planted on earth, and provide an interesting counterpoint to the grace of the modern pieces, but they are only secondary delights. It is the latter which rule.

made by Borge Mogensen and the shelving, by the designer and teacher Mogens Kock, dates back the thirties.

So it is that in this house each chair and each table has first and last names. The famous valet chair in the guest rooms is fascinating. Little by little, the "old bachelor" – as it is called – unfolds and shows off its complexity. Its back, for example, is the most anatomical of hangers for gentlemen's suit jackets; and the chair seat lifts up to hang the pants and render them wrinkle-proof. The modest drawer that appears when the seat rises is the perfect place for wallet, handkerchief, cufflinks and other extras spewed out by pockets. When the King of Denmark visited the Danish furniture show in 1953, he not only greatly admired the chair, but also ordered eight of them. So the fine, arduous labor of Hans J. Wegner, who had worked 48 hours in a row with his operator to have the chair ready for the fair, bore fruit and was happily rewarded. King Frederik IX and Queen Ingrid must have felt the same when they inaugurated this, the official Danish seat in Washington, on the 12th of October 1960.

ECUADOR

Once upon a time there was a ship captain named Thomas Moran, who dreamed of owning a Classical Revival-style home in the nation's capital. One fine day in 1942 he woke up and made up his mind. He commissioned Victor de Mers to design him one on Bancroft Place, just around the corner from his then residence. He was immersed in this project when the U. S. Navy ordered him to Puerto Rico to assume the position of Chief of Staff of the Tenth Naval District. Although Captain Moran and his wife Elma were permanent fixtures on the capital's social scene, the duty-bound officer immediately accepted. But he also decided to follow through with the construction. This decision turned into good luck and good fortune for the architect, and not only in monetary terms. The residence was awarded the Washington Board of Trade for Municipal Art prize for the best-designed home of 1942.

And once upon a time there was a country in the northwest of South America called Ecuador, which in 1944 was looking for a new residence in the capital for its ambassadors. And of all the beautiful homes they visited in Washington, the one they liked best was the one with an elegant and imposing façade, a graceful staircase and an elegant back garden. And it belonged to none other than our tale's Captain Moran.

And because every fairy tale worth the telling must have its prince, ours could not lack one. And in this case it was the then ambassador, Galo Plaza, who discharged his duties in a princely fashion. His personal characteristics and professionalism joined together to make a positive impact on this capital. He personally took charge of furnishing the house, a project which took him two years. In 1948, when the residence was already a beautiful, concrete and well-inaugurated reality, Plaza assumed the presidency of Ecuador.

He would be succeeded by important diplomats, among them his son-in-law Ricardo Crespo Zaldumbide, Mario Ribadeneira, Francisco Illescas, Augusto Dillon, Luis Antonio Peñaherrera, José Ricardo Chiriboga, Alejandro Ponce Luque, Neptalí Ponce, José Antonio Correa, Gustavo Larrea, Carlos Mantilla, Alberto Quevedo Toro, José Corsino Cárdenas, Gustavo Icaza Borja, Rafael García Velasco (ex-Foreign Minister), Jaime Moncayo, Edgar Terán (ex-Foreign Minister), Alberto Maspons and Ivonne A-Baki. They all left their marks, they all came and then they all went. Not so the exquisite and precious pair of Quito School Virgins that, to this day and from their places on the wall of the staircase, keep watch over the home and greet its visitors.

It would be impossible to imagine a more appropriate greeting. As soon as you get a glimpse of them, you ask: where do these marvels come from? The answer leads to the subject of Ecuador's Colonial Era treasures: its churches and convents; the School of Quito; the American Baroque; and the motif of the Virgin Mary. The most important source of inspiration for 17th and 18th century artists was the Virgin Mary, and more specifically, the Immaculate Conception or Purísima, a passion inherited from Spain. The works by artists such as Miguel de Santiago, Manuel de Samaniego and Bernardo de Legarda are spoken of with a reverential admiration. The canvas of Sagrada Familia con niño en pañales (Sacred Family with Child in Diapers) elicits no less fervor. An anonymous painting from the 19th century, this depiction of the sacred family is a paradigm of religious syncretism. The mestizaje or mixing

A pair of important columns flanks the entrance hall. In the background there is a 17th century canvas of the Virgin Mary from the School of Quito. She was the source of inexhaustible inspiration for the artists of the 17th and 18th centuries. Works by such painters as Miguel de Santiago, Manuel de Samaniego and Bernardo de Legarda are mentioned with reverential admiration.

of races and religions is embodied in the colored panels that wrap the infant, a faithful reproduction of the swaddling clothes used by the indigenous peoples of the country.

Pre-Columbian Ecuador dominates the study, thanks to the recovery, in the 1980s, here in the United States, of an important lot of burial-ground objects stolen from the nation. Today, they have taken over the library shelves and their variety and perfection is an invitation to immerse yourself in the history of the venuses of the Valdivian culture (3500 B. C.), the Machalilla ware (1800 B. C.), and the figures of the Chorrera culture (1500-500 B. C.). Through them we are reminded that knowledge and the arts did not begin in Ecuador in the 15th century. Although Ecuador had many golden years during the Colonial Era, they prove that its history started much earlier, as the embassy's pre-Columbian ceramic collection amply proves.

EUROPEAN COMMISSION

Even today, when it is surrounded by other grand homes, this residence commands our attention. Imagine the impact of this Classical Revival villa when it was built in 1922 and was the only structure on the block! And so it remained until 1940. The mansion was a pioneer in what would become the historic and fashionable neighborhood of Sheridan-Kalorama. The choice of location speaks well of the foresight of the home's original owner, builder and first resident, the developer Michael A. Weller. He only lived in the house until 1926.

The European Commission acquired the home in 1970 and it became a center of Washington's diplomatic life. Its previous owner, C. Douglas Dillon, bought it in 1957, when he was Under Secretary of State in the Eisenhower administration. Dillon was known for his frequent entertaining of Washington's political elite during his stay in the residence from 1957 until 1970. He was one of the founders of the Inter-American Development Bank and became Secretary of the Treasury under President Kennedy.

In her book *Personal History*, Katherine Graham retells an interesting anecdote about President Kennedy's nomination of C. Douglas Dillon as Secretary of the Treasury. According to the former publisher of the *Washington Post*, Kennedy had asked her husband to go personally to Dillon and inform him of the President's wishes. Even though an elegant dinner party was in progress at the Belmont Road residence, the task was so pressing that it couldn't wait until the next day. The loyal messenger arranged for the butler to leave open a dressing room window, which allowed him to crawl in during the party and inform Dillon of the president's wishes. The Dillons decorated the drawing room with 18th century French-style *trompe l'oeil* murals, one of their many efforts to enhance the home's aesthetic.

The original conception of the house was the work of the well-known architect, William Lawrence Bottomley. In 1996 the European Commission started a major refurbishing of the mansion. We may call it an addition, an expansion or a *risorgimento*. One of the first improvements was the enlargement of the drawing room, which was done by transforming an outside interior patio into an enclosed room, thus creating a new light-filled space known as the garden room. The dining room was not only expanded to twice its original size, but was also given a coffered ceiling and three arched French doors which open onto the interior patio. The penthouse was renovated as well, changing from a small room to a guest suite with a sitting room, two bedrooms and two bathrooms. We cannot fail to mention the view, overlooking the fascinating garden, fountain and sculptures. It shows the admiration that Innocenti and Webel, the landscape architects, shared for Italianate parks. Webel also designed the gardens at Blair House, where the White House hosts foreign dignitaries.

In terms of *risorgimento*, none was more applauded than the restoration, in all of their majesty and glory, of the original colors of the exterior walls, an incomparable rose-terracotta. When Ambassador Günther Burghardt and his wife Rita Byl return to Europe

During the last renovation, the dining room was not only expanded to double its original size, but it was also given a coffered ceiling with recessed lighting and three arched French doors which open onto the interior patio.

Opposite page
*The gardens are proof of the
admiration and fascination
that Innocenti and Webel,
the landscape architects,
shared for Italianate parks.
Webel also designed the
gardens at Blair House,
where the White House
hosts foreign dignitaries.*

Right
*The drawing room was
enlarged by transforming
an outside interior patio
into the garden room.
In the middle, over the
mosaic floor, is an art déco
coffee table made from the
cast-iron window of a
Chicago bank. In the back,
a painting by the Ukrainian
artist Serhiy Savchenko,
born in 1972.*

with their valuable and varied art collection, the house may lose a great deal of its current interest. But any future diplomat should be forbidden to touch the house's color. For it is that pale rose, with the flavor of the Mediterranean, which stands as the coat of arms of the 15 European countries that call this residence their home.

Left

The sculpture by Maurice Pomeranc (a Belgian, born in Poland in 1919) contrasts with and balances the other pieces in the room: the antique 19th century Victorian breakfront, the mahogany table and chairs, and the late-19th century mirror. In back, an 18th century screen with four painted leather panels.

Above

Ambassador Günther Burghardt and his wife Rita Byl have made themselves at home by bringing in an important part of their valuable art collection. Over the chimney hangs Autumn Light in Brabant, *by the Belgian painter Ward Lernout. A European glass collection rests on the built-in wall cupboards. Next to the window is Bram Bogart's* Venetian Blind. *Two other equally spectacular paintings by the same artist hang in the dining room.*

125

FRANCE

No one would expect to see the French flag flying at this ambassadorial residence, which has been variously described as neo-Tudor, Norman, Vanderbilt and Jacobean. But there the flag has flown since 1936, when the French government bought the mansion for the residence of its ambassadors.

With its splendid location and magnificent furnishings, the house was meant to reign over the city. Built in 1910, it was designed by the architect Henri de Sibour for the millionaire William W. Lawrence. He then sold it to another millionaire's millionaire, John Hays Hammond, who transformed it into the obligatory meeting place for the important personalities of the era.

Hammond was a kind of King Midas of the late 19th and early 20th centuries. He amassed his prodigious fortune here – in the gold mines of California – and there – in the diamond mines of the South African Transvaal. He was an erudite philanthropist, and in 1909 this Californian decided to establish his residence in the U.S. capital. A personal friend of President William Howard Taft, he was sent as his envoy to King George V's coronation in England, just one of the many appointments he held in his life.

In 1917, he bought the Kalorama Avenue mansion from Lawrence – with its fabulous view of Rock Creek Park and the Taft Bridge – for $ 400 000. He was a grand collector and after every trip valuable *objets d'art* would be added to the décor of the house. Among them was a set of Empire furniture, some pieces of which can still be admired today in the principal salons of the embassy residence.

A Gallic diplomat said that, in large part, it was precisely the fine French antiques in the house that motivated his country to purchase the residence. The façade, his wife quipped, "could well belong to a Scottish baron." What led Hammond to sell it to France and not to Brazil, which also bid on the house, is yet another story.

In 1931, the popular and hyper-social Natalie Hammond died after suffering from sleeping sickness. Three months later, her disconsolate widower shut the doors of the magnificent property and with his children left Washington forever. Hammond is said to have wandered until his death, traveling between his properties in Florida and Massachusetts. A month before his death, he closed the deal with the French government. It was only when ambassador André de Laboulaye and his wife moved in – abandoning the former French embassy residence on 16th street, on the old Embassy Row – that the mansion's doors were opened again. And how!

There then began that the much-lauded melding between the furnishings acquired from the Hammonds, those contributed by the French Republic – Gobelin tapestries, paintings, silver, fine rugs, tables and lamps –, and the personal touches that each diplomat adds to the residence.

Since then, the dining room has been enlarged and the land adjacent to the embassy residence purchased. The mansion's neighbors, who had feared that a tall building would be erected on the empty lot, breathed a collective sigh of relief at the purchase. According

The 17th century paintings by Noel Coypel (on loan from Versailles) and the Louis XIV clock are the principal pieces in the dining room's décor.

Left
*"Visually speaking, this is
a transition room between
the house and garden," says
the Ambassador's spouse.
In a recent redecoration, the
whole of this luminous and
modern salon was furnished
with pieces from France.*

Above
*A 19th century walnut desk,
is the centerpiece of the
Salon des Boiseries.*

Salon des Boiseries.

to Ambassador Henri-Hayes, who was charged with the acquisition of the lot, the green space that a mansion of such proportions required had finally become a reality. Unfortunately, in 1942, as the ambassador was about to realize his dream of clearing the lot, Secretary of State Cordell Hull, without much ceremony, asked the then representative of the Vichy government to pack his bags and go back to France. From 1942 to1945, when De Gaulle appointed his Minister of Information, Henri Bonnet, to the post, the residence was shuttered; during that time it was managed by the Swiss government.

If Hélène Bonnet made a lasting mark as a hostess, the stay of Claude Alphand was no less important. The first wife of ambassador Hervé Alphand, Claude spared no effort to lighten and renew the décor of the embassy residence. The dark and heavy wood paneling became cream-colored, and paintings by Bonnard, Marquet and Poliakoff replaced the somber and discolored tapestries. No chronicler of the period fails to mention how Mme. Alphand's original floral arrangements, which mixed fresh and artificial flowers with a sure touch, set a precedent for such floral designs in the city. The social whirl nevertheless worn out the efficient ambassador's wife, who ceded her place to Nicole, the second Mme. Alphand.

Her incomparable beauty, talent and charisma remain unforgettable to those who knew her – this was the gracious concert of gifts that led *Time* magazine to put her on its cover. Equally impressive was her cool self-possession when the house caught fire on a freezing February night after an electrical short-circuit. What the fire did not ruin, the firemen's hoses rendered unusable. Only after the flames were under control did Mme. Alphand, whose servants thought she would be moving into a five-star hotel, say goodnight and retire to her smoky bedroom. The fast and close friendship she formed with Jacqueline Kennedy, the then First Lady, is also fondly remembered.

Below, left

This staircase, originally darker, was lightened to make the entrance hall brighter. In the background, the "Africa" tapestry and a portrait of Lafayette.

Below, right

Entrance hall with console table and Louis XIV mirror.

Also memorable was the five-year stay of Emanuel (Bobby) and Hélène de Margery. It is no secret that the French embassy residence was never so French as in those years, thanks to the great style of the ambassadorial couple and the valuable collection of personal objects the pair brought with them.

It is a well-known fact that, what with charity events, official dinners and working lunches, the doors of these diplomatic mansions are never closed. Never is there a bigger event in an ambassador's residence than a visit from its country's president. This fact is proven time and again, on an almost daily basis, in Washington, and was confirmed for the French embassy residence when De Gaulle arrived for President Kennedy's state funeral in 1963, and, once more, on President Miterrand's state visit in the 80s.

France's house on a hill, "the most ambassadorial mansion of all the embassy mansions in this capital", as someone wisely called it, enters the 21st century with the same elegant presence it had at its birth, nearly a century ago. Commanding the ship today, as she has done so ably throughout the past six and a half years, is Anne Bujon de l'Estang, the modern and sophisticated spouse of the ambassador of the French Republic to the United States. In the redecorated living room of the mansion, the only "casual" space in the residence, the brick and white tones, the rugs, the curtains and the always-fresh flower arrangements (found throughout the mansion), all reflect her distinctive style.

Empire salon. In the background, a painting by *Pierre Bonnard,* Coin de Fenêtre, *property of the Louvre Museum.*

GERMANY

For those who like symmetry, order, and rationality, an earthly paradise has arrived in the form of the German Ambassador's residence. Indeed, in this house, everything has a reason for being – the door, rug, screen, woodcut and "mocca" set; the staircases, semi-circular chairs and lamps; the magnolias and the very air, earth and water. Better yet, everything was conceived at the same time. Nothing is a product of mere whim. The diplomats who inhabit the residence in turn are not expected to put their mark on, intervene with or alter the established aesthetic.

One thing is the house of a normal, everyday citizen and quite another, the official residence of the German representative. In the former, the owner is free to place what he wants where he wants it and to decorate as he pleases. In the latter, the building is an integral part of the image that a country like Germany – which has a millenniums-old cultural tradition – displays in a capital like Washington. The embassy residence has to fully illustrate the importance that the Federal Republic of Germany gives to its relationship with the United States.

The prestigious architect Oswald Mathias Ungers kept all of this firmly in mind when he submitted his project to the architectural competition that chose the design of the new diplomatic seat. And it was also critical for the jury which, in 1988, weighed the proposals submitted by a group of professionals of equal renown. Among the many varied trends and architectural styles in Germany, the winning design stood out for the way that it combined tradition and modernism in equal measure.

No one should have been surprised by the holistic work method Professor Ungers utilized in the project, which placed even the most minimal details under his control – it was his usual way of working. From its very conception, a multidisciplinary team of artists collaborated in the design of the building. So that when the time came to hang the 12 woodcuts on canvas by Markus Lupertz on the top third of the walls of the great reception hall – the most imposing room in the building – the exact place for each one was already known. A similar thing happened with Gerhard Merz's entrance-hall wall paintings, as well as Christa Naher's four paintings, which use earth, air, fire and water as their central motif. Ungers had already reserved the corners of the gentlemen's sitting room for her paintings, knowing full well that his formal, orderly architectural style would form an interesting contrast with the mystical images of the painter and give the space a special ambiance.

In the so-called "ladies'room", the strategy was different. Here the starring roles were taken by the circular design of the ceiling and the rug. Everything is by Rosemarie Trockel: a symphony of greens and browns. Even the china was designed for the purpose of maintaining the unity and establishing a perfect harmony with the tones that come in from the garden through the great glass windows.

Ungers is never content with just "a simple lamp", if it can resemble and be sculpture as well. The ones that discreetly light this residence become luminous, functional works of arts. The same principle applies to the magnificent red lacquer screen by Simon Ungers,

The great reception hall is, without a doubt, the most imposing space in this impressive building. A glass wall connects it to a terrace that overlooks the park

Opposite page
Designed as a ladies' sitting room, this space may, on occasion, become a more informal and intimate dining area. Here the starring roles are taken by the circular design of the ceiling and the rug. Everything is by Rosemarie Trockel, everything is in green and coffee. Even the china is designed to maintain the unity and establish a perfect harmony with the tones that come in from the garden through the great windows.

Right
A small library that is connected to the reception hall.

that divides the great dining room into one, two or three spaces, depending on the number of guests. Whether folded or unfolded, (it stands as a column when not in use), it is a marvelous piece.

The guiding hand of the architect reached into each and every room of the public spaces of the residence. But not into the wing reserved for the family quarters. These are private rooms, and as such, individuality is permitted in them.

Dr. Bernhard Korte created the architectural concepts used for the exterior. A double set of stairs runs downhill through the park, respecting the slope of the land. Finally, a reflecting pool mirrors the compact structure. Assuming it had existed back then, what would it have reflected when the Harriman villa stood on this hill?

Left

A smaller entrance hall precedes the reception hall. According to Ungers, its architect, the residence in Washington " …is neither a castle nor a manor, but a complex mechanism for diverse functions, duties and requirements." Among others, it serves as a representational building, a private residence, an office and the site of official ceremonies.

Above

A frieze of twelve paintings occupies the upper third of the two long, facing walls. They are by the artist Markus Lupertz and belong to the series "Men Without Women – Parsifal." They were specially made for the niches.

A screen of wood, red lacquer and steel, by Simon Ungers, serves to divide the immense L-shaped dining room into large or small spaces, depending on the number of guests.

GUATEMALA

You are unlikely to hear those who live in this great residence complain about a lack of green space. Even though it is not located in the middle of the jungle like the magnificent Mayan archeological site of *Tikal,* it does enjoy the abundant lushness of neighboring Rock Creek Park. It was built in 1919, in the post-war era when many other mansions went up in this exclusive zone, and the Government of Guatemala purchased it in 1960. The building creates an unusual feeling in the heart of the visitor. The embassy home is decorated with a minimum of paintings, textiles and other Mayan objects: a very counterintuitive style decision, when one considers the incomparable beauty of the country, its millenary culture and rich handicraft traditions.But the choice of objects has the virtue of forcing one to think about and continue to investigate that culture. The artifacts act, in a certain way, as *aperitifs* and invite you to discover the country of a thousand marvels.

The paintings signal the first route into the country. The oil portrait in the entrance hall places us squarely before Francisco Marroquín (1478-1563), the notable priest who arrived in Guatemala in 1528, along with Pedro de Alvarado, the conqueror of the land. Four years later, the Queen of Spain named him Bishop of the Province of Guatemala, with the title of "Protector of the Indians." He was a visionary who discovered that the only way to educate and convert the Indians and teach them Christian doctrine was to do so in their native tongue. He himself learned *quiché* and taught the first instructors in indigenous languages. He wrote a catechism in *quiché,* which was published in Mexico and Guatemala. He even authored a study guide for the prelates, called "The Art of Learning the Languages of Guatemala." And we are speaking here of the 16th century. What if Bishop Marroquín had not concerned himself with this aspect of the Church's mission? Five hundred years later, twenty-four Mayan tongues are still spoken and their speakers represent 40% of the Guatemalan population. For them the native languages and the ancient *Cholq'ij* calendar have never lost their validity.

In the same entrance hall, the Guatemalan artist Andrés Curruchiche brings to the fore the importance of corn, the staple of the Guatemalan diet, in his *"Mujeres Alimentando con Maíz las Gallinas"* (Women Feeding Corn to the Hens). The New World origin of the maize plant has never been doubted, but the country's people affirm that, more than American, the corn stalk is Guatemalan. The *Popol Vuh,* the ancient Mayan-Quiché sacred text written by an anonymous indigenous author, tells that the Creators *Gucumatz* and *Tepeu,* bored by their failed attempts to create man first from mud and then from wood, found the magic formula when they formed him from cornmeal. "So that the new beings spoke, saw, walked, took things…and were granted intelligence."

In the dining room, a third painting speaks to us of *Antigua* or *Santiago de los Caballeros de Guatemala,* also known as "the Jewel of America." It became the second capital of the country in 1542, after a flood devastated *Ciudad Vieja* (the "Old City"). But Antigua did not enjoy its luck forever. The terrible earthquake of 1773 caused the governor to relocate the capital in the *Valle de la Ermita,* where Guatemala City stands today. Antigua

A series of lithographs by the well-known Guatemalan artist Frederick Crocker hang over the dining room sideboard. The dining room table's tablecloth is a good example of the Guatemalan people's dexterity in spinning, knitting and combining colors.

Page 144
Paintings accompany the Louis XIV-style furnishings of the drawing room. An oil of Mariano Galvez (President from 1831 to 1838) hangs over the sofa. He was a prominent lawyer. The improvement of the public education system, the founding of the National Library and National Museum, and the establishment of civil marriage were among his legacies.

Page 145
The portraits on the walls of the residence are an homage to the great men of the country. Here we see one of Bishop Francisco Marroquín (1478-1563), who arrived in Guatemala in 1528 with its conqueror Pedro de Alvarado.

emerged from its lethargy two hundred years later, in the wake of the prosperity brought by coffee cultivation, and today it is a Unesco "Cultural Patrimony of Humanity" site. The city has been carefully renovated and reconstructed. Each convent, mansion, church, fountain, patio, stone archway, wall and roof has been meticulously restored, revealing the glorious architectural past that leaves all who visit it in awe.

But the Mayas are not the only ones who forged Guatemala's riches. Nature endowed it with a remarkable geography and fauna. The former is referred to in the Hilary Arathoon painting which hangs in the drawing room, *Lago Amatitlán* (Lake Amatitlán), and the latter in the Fortuny oil, *Quetzal* – considered the most beautiful bird in the world – that hangs in the studio. The painting in the family room depicts the famous Central Plaza of Chichicastenango, a Maya-Quiché village located half an hour from Lake Atitlán, where one of the most picturesque and fascinating markets in the Americas is held every Thursday and Sunday. It is also the place where, in an inspired syncretism, the native population, gathering in its Colonial-period churches, combines Catholic rituals with the religious practices of their Mayan ancestors.

HOLY SEE

Those who walk by Embassy Row and notice the papal shield carved on this residence's entrance can never imagine what vicissitudes it endured before it could get to its rightful place. This is all part of history now but the apostolic delegates – they only started to be called Nuncios in 1984, after the United States government, under Ronald Reagan, officially established diplomatic relations with the Holy See – lived in three different places before the pontifical representative's residence was finished in 1939.

The last place they occupied was on Biltmore street, and it was precisely the increasingly commercial character of this address that led a group of American high prelates to consider the possibility of building their own seat. A committee of bishops, presided over by the Archbishop of Baltimore, Michael J. Curley, was created for this purpose.

It has been well said that it was hard to know who the exact "client" was. After reading the history of its construction, it is abundantly clear that the achievement would have been even harder without the work of Monsignor Curley. The Monsignor was present and active from its beginnings and he persisted in making a go of it against all odds. The odds were the health problems that plagued him, the difficulty of fund-raising in the middle of the Great Depression and the criticisms provoked by the magnificence of the project.

Fortunately, Curley was able to count on the support of the apostolic delegates every step of the way. These were Archbishop Pietro Fumasoni-Biondi, who was there to purchase the lot in 1931 and oversee the drafting of the plans, and his successor Archbishop Amleto Cicognani, who, while he had the honor to preside over the inauguration of the residence, also shed his share of bitter tears during its construction. Monsignor Curley never doubted the development possibilities of the Massachusetts Avenue lot when it came time to choose the land. There was a reason why the British had built their embassy across the street (in 1928), he argued. The Archbishop had a keen eye. Today, this stretch of Massachusetts Avenue between Dupont Circle and the National Cathedral is known as Embassy Row. And if that weren't enough, the residence of the Vice-President of the United States is located exactly across the street from the Holy See's.

The search for the architect began immediately after the land was purchased. Frederick Vernon Murphy, an American architect and Roman Catholic who had studied at the École des Beaux Arts in Paris, was chosen. Murphy had an impressive professional curriculum: he had built the Basilica of the Sacred Heart on 16th Street in 1919, among other buildings.

He was the founder of the architecture department at the Catholic University of America in 1911 and this is said to have weighed heavily in his favor, as Curley was a big supporter of the institution.

Then came the complex and difficult stage of raising funds for the construction of the residence. It could not be modest or small, given the diverse functions it had to serve. It had to be the home and office of the apostolic delegate; it had to have a chapel, reception halls, and guest rooms for any ecclesiastical authorities passing through the capital. Additionally, it had to have quarters for the residence personnel.

A magnificent staircase leads to the second floor. Light seeps through everywhere and is multiplied by the stained-glass windows. Some reproduce scenes from Dante's Divine Comedy.

The warmth of the chapel, located on the first floor, balances the severity of the other rooms. It is a small miracle of light that inspires devotion.

So while Murphy pondered the exact style to give the building, obstacles and temptations lay ahead. A new lot was offered to the project in 1934. Many wavered, but not Curley, who said that it would be "better to stay on Biltmore than to sell the Massachusetts Avenue land." He supported his choice by insisting than never again in their life could they buy a better or cheaper lot. A short while later, the work had to come to a complete stop, due to lack of funds. Monsignor would not go forward without the money in hand, because he did not want to be "left with all the weight on his shoulders" at the end of the project. He had a profound understanding of the human soul and he knew that, by using the right arguments at the precise time, the money would be raised. He threw himself into this delicate task, body and soul. No letter went unsent and no Catholic door failed to receive a knock. As a result of his efforts, at the end of 1937, Murphy received orders to proceed with the work.

Paintings by Italian artists and portraits of Cardinals and Popes adorn the walls.

A possibility that hadn't even been remotely considered came up before the building was finished: that of acquiring the adjacent lot to prevent any "inappropriate neighbors" from moving in next door. The apostolic delegate thought this was a sensible proposal until he saw the size of the land. He discarded the possibility there and then. Nevertheless, anonymous donors – only afterwards was it known that it had been Cardinal Dougherty, aided by the very same Curley – resolved the situation and the land on the corner of Massachusetts Avenue and 34th Street was added to the site.

On March 27th, 1939, the Vatican delegation moved into their new residence and on April 25th it was formally inaugurated with a reception. Curley had again got his way: he wanted to avoid any type of celebration when the first stone was laid. In his judgment, the ceremony had to wait until each and every stone was in its place. And that is the way it was.

Murphy was educated in the École des Beaux Arts and he closely adhered to the classical concepts he learned there: purity of line, symmetry, equilibrium and refinement in the details. This room, with its high windows that overlook Massachusetts Avenue, has them all in abundance.

ICELAND

The personal history of the original owners of ambassadorial mansions of the capital – of why they moved to Washington, how they made their fortunes, what they were famous for – plays a transcendent role in the aura of their houses. It is further enhanced when you add to the mix the life and works of the (usually famous) architects and designers of the houses. In the case of the Embassy of Iceland, by contrast, which was built in 1928 by an owner who became wealthy through real estate, a "former tenant" and its current owners of record merit the spotlight. Even today, one of the most memorable details about this residence, located in the exclusive Kalorama neighborhood, is its association with Madame Chiang Kai-Shek, who used it as a temporary base when she visited Washington. Intelligent, charismatic and highly cultured, she was considered the direct envoy of her husband, the Generalissimo, before the government of the United States. Despite her lack of an official portfolio or government title, she held this position for a number of reasons, including her perfect command of English.

But people also remember a less than rosy detail of her time at the mansion: the removal of two sustaining beams, the result of her decision to enlarge the reception rooms. The government of Iceland, which bought the house for the residence of its ambassadors in 1964, was forced to close it for repairs between 1996 and 1998, because it was sinking.

These days, in 2002, the greenery of Rock Creek Park is visible – as it was then – but now the high-quality works of Icelandic artists cover the walls. And it is here that Bryndís Schram, the spouse of the current ambassador, plays a role that, in an appropriate proportion, is as central as the one played by Madame Chiang in former times.

When speaking of her native land, this Icelandic actress, writer and TV personality points out that it is not as cold as Washington and that it was the English (after the Middle Ages) who named it Iceland, not its inhabitants. Before then, it had been "Island", the "Isle of God" in Gaelic (the Irish language). She adds that "probably that version is not true, but I like it. It makes it easier to sell the image of my country, never cold and never hot. The minimum temperature in winter is about 28 degrees and in the summertime, in general it is about 52 degrees." This is why she uses the heated pool in her current residence throughout the year.

Of the house's former inhabitants, very little remains. The one exception is the master bedroom's furniture set, which was a a wedding gift from Ambassador Thor Thors to his beautiful daughter. Three years later, the girl killed herself and the Icelandic government bought it from her mother, by then widowed. "She must have been an enchanting young girl, "says Madame Schram, "her ghost certainly is."

The embassy's policy of making Iceland better known every day has a palpable effect: there is never a month in which this diplomatic seat does not host an art exhibition, a concert, an author reading or a fashion show. This always includes a gastronomic event, featuring lamb, herring, cod, salmon, lobster, scallops, and pancakes with cream and blueberry marmalade. More than houses inhabited by diplomats, these residences are veritable showcases of their countries, and Iceland's is an excellent example of it.

Over the chimney in the drawing room, Apollo 13, by Erro, "one of the few Icelandic artists who is famous outside of Iceland, he lives and paints in Paris," recounts Bryndis Schram, wife of the current ambassador. "It shows the astronauts visiting Iceland to train before their journey into space. Our country, which has a lot of lava, seems like what we tend to think the Earth originally looked like. In the center of the painting, Louis XV and a mannequin resembling Marilyn Monroe stand out: stars from different centuries."

Opposite page
The embassy's policy of making Iceland better known every day has a palpable effect: there is never a month in which this diplomatic seat does not host an art exhibition, a concert, an author reading or a fashion show. More than houses inhabited by diplomats, these residences are showcases of their countries, and Iceland's is an excellent example.

Above
The paintings – these two and some others are on loan from the National Gallery of Art in Iceland – comprise the central decorative feature of the dining room. To the right, Sunrise at Two a.m. *is by Hringur Johannesson and* Woman, *on the left is the work of Sigurdur Örlygsson.*

Left
*The principal painting
in the dining room
is by Jón Stefánsson,
an early-20th century
landscape painter.*

Opposite page
*A work by the
Icelandic sculptor
Gudrun Halldorsdottir.*

INDIA

The Indian Government's decision to purchase the Macomb Street residence in May 1945 was an outstanding one. The exact figures are unknown; what we do know is that it paid a fraction of what it cost its original owner to restore. Walter Horton Schoellkopf, a U.S. career diplomat, bought it in 1930 and by the time he finished refurbishing the mansion he had spent close to a million dollars.

But he was not lacking for money. His grandfather, Jacob Schoellkopf, hailed from Buffalo, New York and had been a pioneer in the hydraulic energy sector. He was also a prosperous businessman. The family had originally emigrated from Germany in 1842 and legend has it that the first Schoellkopf left his native village when told he had to tip his hat to the mayor. "If that is so, I am going to America," was his answer.

The residence, named *"La Quinta"*, is set high above Rock Creek Park among tall trees and located just off Connecticut Avenue. The house was transformed into a refined Georgian-style mansion in a renovation entrusted to Ward Brown, the same architect who designed the current Embassy of Holland, and to the builder R. W. Bolling, the brother of Woodrow Wilson's second wife. The renovations lasted a year and were so thorough that almost nothing was left of the original structure. The red bricks used to cover the façade were about the only materials that were not imported. They were made in Baltimore, Maryland, and based on samples of antique English brickwork.

The front door, the iron grillwork and marble entrance came from an old house in London. The mantelpiece in the sunroom came from Dorchester Mansion, also in London. Two large wings were added to the dining and sitting rooms. The intricate 150-year-old parquet in the salon came from a French château and was laid down in 1931. And because things had to be done perfectly from beginning to end, two artisans from Paris were specially flown in to Washington for the installation. The mirrors were cut in two sections before they were hung, in order to preserve the authenticity of the Louis XV style.

Each *objet d'art* was imported from somewhere in Europe. The odd pieces, such as a fireback dating from the First World War, came from the chimney of a bishop's home in Verdun, France. The diplomat had spent some time in that region and brought it home as a souvenir. The thick mahogany doors and wood paneling on the walls of the dining room are English, as is the frame on the mirror, which bears the unmistakable stamp of the school of Grinling Gibbons, the famous English woodcarver (1648-1720).

The Schoellkopfs took great pains in refurbishing the residence and when the mansion was inaugurated in 1931, with a reception to honor the Ambassador of Spain and his wife, hosts and guests agreed that the effort had been well worth it.

Curiously, the homeowners did not occupy the residence for long, and it was rented out for years to notable personalities. Among the prominent tenants were Joseph E. Davies, ex-Ambassador of the United States to the Soviet Union and Belgium (Mrs. Davies later became Mrs. Merriweather Post); William Hartman Woodin, Secretary of the Treasury in Franklin Delano Roosevelt's first term; and Colonel Robert Guggenheim, Eisenhower's Ambassador to Portu-

The cheerful and inviting ballroom, done up in Louis XV décor with mirrors and gilding, lends an air of grandeur and opulence to the space and combines the best of Indian and European styles. The antique parquet came from a French château and was 150 years-old when it was installed, in 1931, by two artisans who were specially flown in from Paris. The beautiful crystal chandeliers are from France and were brought in 1930. The striking bronze Nataraj or "Dancing Shiva" statue is an antique from South India and the handmade carpets from India are over 60 years-old. The silver pots in the foreground are handmade, with inscribed designs.

Opposite page

The beautiful wood paneling was brought from England in the early 20th century and the wall chandeliers are from Paris. At the Ambassador's residence, dinner is served on silver plates or thalis.
A traditional thali *meal can include rice, curries,* pappad *(a thin crispy bread), and chutney and pickles.
Curries are usually served in silver bowls or* katoris.

Right

This painting, by the contemporary Indian artist Gogi Saroj Pal, is from the ambassador's personal collection, and is juxtaposed with a sandstone sculpture of Shiva and Parvati that dates back to the 11th century.

gal. Due to his profession, Schoellkopf spent long periods outside the country (he was U.S. Ambassador in Madrid), and after his long illness, the family moved to another residence in 1940. Sir Girja Shankar Bajpai, the future Secretary General of the Ministry of Foreign Relations of India, leased the residence in 1942, when his country was still under British rule. A talented diplomat, he spent six years in Washington as his country's first representative and made a strong impact on Roosevelt. He was a lover of painting, rugs and flowers and he himself tended the garden on Macomb Street.

Bajpai paved the way for his country's fine purchase in 1945. Over the years the residence has become a veritable showcase for ancient Indian art treasures, notably a 17th century stone statue of Lord Ganesh in the foyer, a 10th century stone sculpture of Shiva and Parvati, and two exquisite bronze statues of Shiva-Nataraj in the public rooms. Interspersed with the matchless statuary is a happy blend of modern and classical Indian paintings, ranging from miniatures of the Rajasthan and Kishengarh schools to works by contemporary Indian artists like Paramjit Singh, Francis Newton Souza, M.F. Husain and Satish Gujral.

Left

*The gold silk drapes
complement the gilding
on the walls. The former
owner of the residence
brought the fireback from
a bishop's house in Verdun,
France, during World War I.
The antique silver bracelets
in the foreground, from
Orissa in Eastern India, are
from the personal collection
of ambassador Mansingh's
family, as is the Buddhist
thangka from Bhutan on
the far right. The windows
overlook Rock Creek Park.*

Above

*Sunlight streams through the
windows of the sunroom all
day. The beautiful fireplace
came from Dorchester House
in London. The painting from
Nathadwara in Rajasthan is
known as a Pichhwai and is
based on a Krishna theme.
Over a hundred years old, it is
painted on cloth with vegetable
dyes and is remarkable for its
size and skillful rendering. The
smaller painting, also of Lord
Krishna, is from Tanjore in
South India and is done with
gold leaf and gems. The brass
"Kuttu Velaku" lamps at the
fireplace are from South India.*

INDONESIA

Thomas Walsh literally saw his golden dreams come true. He died at 59, far from the soil and the poverty of his native Ireland, with a fortune so enormous that he could never have imagined it in his youth, not even in his most secret fantasies. He emigrated to the United States at 19, without a penny in his pocket and went west to meet up with his brother. Stricken with "gold fever", like so many people, he was one of the lucky few to strike it rich. He tapped a blessed vein deep in the Rocky Mountains. The mine was called Camp Bird in Ouary, Colorado and it turned out to be one of the richest in the world. Young Thomas picked up gold by the handful, until he reached satiety and opulence. According to documents of the era, Camp Bird produced about five thousand dollars in gold a day! In 1903, he sold it for five million dollars to John Hays Hammond, who was later to purchase the mansion that is the French embassy residence today.

During the period when he was a prospector, Walsh had married Carrie Bell Reed and he wanted their two children to have "a good education and some social life", in his own words. The family moved to Washington in 1897 and in the new century bought the land. By 1903 the construction of the most expensive private residence in the capital was almost finished. It ended up costing $835 000. It automatically became the epicenter of the social life, not only of Dupont Circle but the whole city.

On the clear instructions of the owner, Henry Andersen, a New York architect born and educated in Denmark, designed a four-story *Beaux Arts* mansion of undulating lines, with more than fifty rooms. The materials were brick and limestone. The entrance archway had a piece of gold and iron ore encrusted in it, perhaps to scare away the memory of his lean years. It is estimated that the outlay on Persian rugs, French paintings and decorative objects alone reached two million dollars. The Walshes referred to the house as "the 20/20" (alluding to the address), in order to lower the profile of so much spending and splendor. The most notable interior feature was the principal staircase – it was "Y" shaped –, which brought to mind a steamship deck, and led up to the different floors of the residence and their grand open spaces. A private theater and ballroom, to which one ascended by elevators, occupied the fourth story.

Some say that the palatial mansion was built with King Leopold of Belgium in mind, a personal friend of the Walsh family, who had announced a visit to Washington in 1903 on his way to the St. Louis Exposition. Others say that when they learned of the visit, they spared no expense to build an apartment on the third floor of the residence. It was specially designed and decorated for the King. Although King Leopold was unable to come, his nephew King Albert and Queen Elizabeth did arrive in Washington, D.C. for a three-day visit on October 28, 1919. They were housed in the MacVeagh mansion, which was then the United States government's guest house and is currently the Mexican Cultural Institute.

The bad luck was such that as the royal couple was making their arrival, President Woodrow Wilson suffered a heart attack, which meant that the state dinner could not be held at the White House. Mrs. Walsh graciously offered her residence and the hosts were Vice-Presi-

The most notable interior feature is the grand "Y" – shaped staircase in the middle of the central hall, reminiscent of a steamship deck. It rises to the landing where a marble sculpture of two Roman dancers, part of the original furnishings, sits by the stand where the orchestra used to play during dinners at the mansion.

This replica of King Leopold of Belgium's dining room is a large oak-paneled room decorated in dark green and golden tones. The ceiling is stunning, with a pattern of dark wood quatrefoil, a style popular in 17th century England.

dent and Mrs. Thomas Riley Marshall. The social chronicles of the day mentioned all of the objects on display that had been made from the gold of the Camp Bird mine, from the candelabra to the chrysanthemums and even the plates themselves. Thomas Walsh, who had made it all possible, never knew: he had died nine years before.

His daughter, the very eccentric Evalyn, became a well-known figure in Washington social circles. She was married to Edward McLean, whose family owned *The Washington Post, The Cincinnati Enquirer* and, for a while, *The New York Morning Journal*. She made history, but not just because of her sumptuous lifestyle and the unforgettable parties she and her hus-

Adjoining the ornate Louis XIV Salon, and next to the dining room, is the Organ or Music Room, which gets its name from the massive baroque-style wood organ built into the wall. Also built in are richly-carved wooden cabinets with glass doors which display silverwork, sculpture, batik, and other objets d'art *from various Indonesian islands.*

band gave at "Friendship", the family estate, which is known today as McLean Gardens. She also was famous for owning the fabulous Hope diamond, which she bought from Cartier for $154 000 dollars. The blue-toned Indian diamond is now at the Smithsonian Museum. Evalyn Walsh blamed the many ensuing family tragedies on this famous piece of jewelry.

On her mother's death in 1932, she inherited the mansion, which has been known ever since as the Walsh-McLean house. She occupied the residence for a very short time, and then opted for renting it to various governmental organizations. For ten years, including World War II, she loaned it at no cost to the Washington chapter of the American Red Cross. Evalyn Walsh died in 1947 in another Georgetown home, alone.

The government of Indonesia purchased the residence for its chancery in 1951. When the deal was closed, the Walsh mansion went for a mere $ 335 000, about half a million less than what Thomas Walsh had spent to build it almost half a century earlier. The government spent an additional $75 000 to preserve the massive structure of the mansion and restore the character of the original interior decoration. The first ambassador, Ali Sastroamidjojo, inaugurated the chancery with a reception for five hundred guests.

Little by little, they added some oriental touches, such as the *Garuda* or golden eagle under the threshold. It is a symbol of creative energy. (Gold suggests the grandeur of the nation and black symbolizes nature). Two Balinese stone statues in the entrance hall keep evil away and attract goodness. A new building with additional office space was erected in 1982, and it was annexed to the back part of the mansion. As is fitting, the center stage is occupied by the mansion, which is used today for large receptions. The contrast is evident: the new headquarters is modern, with its simple and pure lines. Passing from one ambiance to the other may be a matter of minutes or… centuries.

Left

From the moment you enter this Louis XIV salon, formerly used as a Drawing Room, you feel the air of prosperity and splendor. Magnificent gold chandeliers hang from the vaulted ceiling. There are also exquisite paintings, like the unsigned "Eternity of Angels". Space is not a problem and today, as in the past, great receptions are held here.

Above

The skylight, with floral motifs on an ochre field, is an artistic touch reminiscent of the late 19th and early 20th century. Situated on the fourth floor, it covers the entire area and illuminates the center of the building.

ITALY

Villa Firenze or Estabrook, the original name given to the current residence of the Italian ambassadors, was born to be the setting for grand social events. It was almost as if Blanche Estabrook O'Brien had had her daughter's debutante ball in mind, if not her wedding, when she chose this marvelous twenty-two acre property, and started the construction in 1925. The house was finished in 1927, and Caroline's debut was in 1929. She married shortly afterwards. What seems odd (or maybe not, given the Depression) was for how short a time they enjoyed it. In 1930, they rented the property to the Minister of Hungary and Madame Pelenyi. The chroniclers of the time talk of the well-attended social events of the Hungarians. But not so of their successor in 1940, George Ghika. During the year that he spent in the house, he led a life in accordance with the historic moment: far from the madding crowd. Mr. and Mrs. Robert Guggenheim became the new owners of the property in 1941. They did not intend to, but circumstances led them to the purchase.

If the truth were told, no one was happier living on his transoceanic yacht, the *Firenze*, than Colonel Guggenheim and his wife Polly. But when the U. S. Navy, invoking the war, asked him for his ship, he did not hesitate for an instant. That is how the couple "anchored" in Estabrook. One of the first measures they took was to re-christen it: from now on the residence at 2800 Albemarle Street would be known as *Firenze House,* in honor of the Colonel's mother, Florence (*Firenze* in Italian), a woman intensely devoted to all things Italian. Then they proceeded to make it into the image and likeness of their good taste, aided by their immense fortune (linked largely to copper). Their basic idea was to give it light; and then, atmosphere. The first was an almost obligatory rite for all new owners of 1920s buildings, which generally tended to be rather gloomy. The Guggenheims started by lightening (bleaching) the color of the wood paneling of the central hall to a pale gray (something similar was done in the French Embassy residence). The organ was changed from gold to silver, so it would not clash.

As to the atmosphere, they arrived at that without changing either the façade of the house or the dimensions of its 59 rooms, nor did they alter the three-story height or the basement (which included something truly exceptional, a bowling alley). No, the atmosphere arrived with the furnishings and the art collections of the new proprietors. For example, it is said that the great fire of 1946 destroyed two Titian paintings and a good quantity of wood paneling on the walls. If the fire had touched the library's panels, the loss would have been incalculable, since they are considered the "treasure" of the mansion. Sir Christopher Wren made them for his own study in 18th century London.

Among the many anecdotes about the redecoration of the house, it is said that Mrs. Guggenheim – an experienced artist – went through seventeen paint samples until she got the blue-gray color she wanted for the principal salon. It was a difficult space, too, because of its large size. What is fascinating about this residence is its handling of space. Every large room is followed by, or includes, another in a more "human scale."

To give a proper atmosphere to the residence, the new owners did not change either the façade of the house or the dimensions of its 59 rooms, nor did they alter the three-story height or the basement (which included something truly exceptional, a bowling alley). No, the atmosphere arrived with the furnishings and the art collections of the new proprietors.

Between the three-story great hall and the enormous drawing room, there is a smaller one, The Rotunda. Its ceiling is highlighted by bas-relief signs of the zodiac and it has an exceptional floor compass made of rare woods and embellished with brass pointers. The principal drawing room also yields its secrets: windows overlooking the gardens create secondary spaces within the principal one. The airy green sunroom or greenhouse is the crowning touch. The Adam-style dining room is considered one of the largest in the capital. At its end, almost flowing into the garden – as if to compensate for such sobriety – we find a warm and more informal dining room.

A smaller room between the three-story-high great hall and the enormous drawing room, the Rotunda has a ceiling highlighted by bas-relief signs of the zodiac. In the center of the floor there is a compass made of rare woods and embellished with brass points.

In 1976 the Italian government bought the mansion. Up until that time, the residence and chancery were one. While the widowed and remarried Polly Logan was moving into her new quarters (and taking with her the stone lions of the terrace, she was a Leo and they had to follow wherever she led), many of the furnishings from the old diplomatic seat began arriving at Villa Firenze, as the mansion was renamed. The rest arrived as

The principal drawing room or il salotto. *The Italianization of the mansion started as soon as Italy acquired the residence.* Villa Firenze *soon welcomed the delicate 19th century Murano chandeliers with matching sconces, the 18th century Venetian-style mirrors and the oils by Bartolomeo Bimbi.*

loans from governmental collections – no small feat since such institutions decline to lend, alleging that the mansions, grand as they may be, do not possess environmental conditions suitable for the conservation of the works they display. There is always a danger that when one asks for the loan to be renewed, the institutions refuse and the works leave, never to return. This has happened more than once.

What has never left the residence, and become a permant feature of Italy's presence, is happiness. The feasts around Blanche Estabrook's pool became the stuff of legend. Indeed, they built the swimming pool before the house went up. By day, they picnicked around the pool; once the sun set the pool was covered with wooden planks and turned into a dance floor, where they danced till dawn.

To be invited to the Tudor-style mansion during the times of the Hungarians and the Guggenheims cemented one's social status. It is not hard to imagine the same thing happening with the "Brunch on the Lawn", even though Anna Maria Salleo, the wife of the current ambassador, speaks of their event in such discreet tones. During the festivities, the embassy showcased the best of Italian cuisine (ten restaurants participated),

Left
*The salotto has its secrets:
bay windows overlooking
the gardens create secondary
spaces within the larger ones,
to form a mixture of formality
and informality that is sober
but not severe.*

Above
*Apart from the library and
the bowling alley, the beauty
of the filtered light created by
the stained-glass windows is
one of the many details that
make this residence unique.*

jewelry and clothing design, wine and cars. Ten Ferraris from different eras were part of the décor. For the Opera Ball – a key fund-raising event in the city – a gondola replaced the Ferraris. The evening's theme was Venice's *Carnevale*.

The District of Columbia's Treasurer must have groaned at the city's loss of revenue when *Firenze House,* a large property-tax contributor, became a diplomatic residence. But the truth is we must be grateful to Blanche Estabrook; her architect, Russell Kluge; the Guggenheims; the Logans; the landscapers; and finally to Italy itself for having the idea of building, furnishing and preserving this house and site.

JAPAN

More than many others, this residence reflects with extreme clarity the soul and traditions of the country it represents – Japan. A pure aesthetic, which teaches that beauty is simple and simplicity is permanent. In the house on Nebraska Avenue, the achievement is grand and shared, because two architects worked on the design process: one from Tokyo, and the other from Watertown, Massachusetts.

The first was Isoya Yoshida, the "brains" behind the project. Of great renown, he studied in Europe and became fascinated with the Italian Renaissance. On returning to his home country, he studied traditional Japanese architecture, and in particular the famous *Sukiya*-style teahouses. He died in 1974, the same year that construction began on the house in Washington.

The second architect was Masao Kinoshita, an American of Japanese descent, and the creator of important designs in the United States. He is most known for his famous *bonsai* Naka Pavilion in the Washington Arboretum, but he has designed other works in New York, Seattle, and Hartford, Connecticut.

The negotiations to secure the site for the Japanese mission began in 1970. It was well known that the size of the embassy staff had swelled – they had begun to rent offices in the Watergate building – and the Ambassador's house on Massachusetts Avenue was needed for the chancery.

The time had come to move. In 1972, they bought the land – for approximately three million dollars – where "Sittie" Parker had lived, ex-wife of the president of the board of directors of the Woodward & Lothrop department store. The building, finished in 1977, is of concrete and stone. Traditional Japanese houses are made from wood and paper, which wouldn't have been very practical under Washington skies.

But all concessions ended there. The roofs are flat and very low to the ground. One never comes to understand it all, but only here does it seem natural for two floors of the house to be at ground level and the others, underground. Only here does it seem logical that the principal structure be connected by a narrow hall to a tea house, called *ochashitsu*, that seems to float on a large pond that is the center of the garden. You suspect that every object has a reason for being: the plants; the rocks; the stone figures half-hidden amongst the ferns; and the trees, some brought from Japan and others grown here without regard for their origins, that mix their leaves in an incessant play of light and shadow. Nor is it easy to explain why the presence of another garden, in a European style, with a pool and a tennis court, never breaks the harmony.

On the inside, each room is in some way an island: the grand salon, a *tempura* room, a guest room, and the principal dining room. Everything is modern in style, of pure lines, and with a minimalist sobriety. Inmense chandeliers, which look more like sculptures, hang from the ceilings and let fall a rain of precious glass. On the walls hang mysterious abstract paintings – in a horizontal format – by famous Japanese artists. Thin paper screens (*shoji*) cover the windows and lend a touch of Japanese classicism.

The foyer, like much of the Ambassador's residence, reflects the stark simplicity of traditional Japanese aesthetics, while incorporating unique contemporary design elements. The chandelier, designed especially for the residence, not only illuminates the room but also enhances its beauty as a work of art. This room is used to greet visitors and to host performances.

The grand salon is an expansive room used for receptions, dinner parties, and performances. On the far wall is displayed "Clouds Arising in the Deep Mountain", by the internationally-renowned artist Kaii Higashiyama. The autumn theme of the salon is spread through the space by using hand-loomed, leaf-patterned wool carpets and a reed motif in the woven wallpaper. The shoji, or sliding paper screens, that cover the windows give the room a classic Japanese touch.

Left and opposite page
One of the most characteristic features of the Ambassador's residence is the ochashitsu, or teahouse. The structure's design uses materials native to Japan, such as Japanese cedar. It is primarily used as a place to demonstrate the tea ceremony to guests at the residence. The captivating Japanese-style garden surrounding the structure is dominated by a large pond, which creates the illusion that the teahouse is floating.

The teahouse and its ceremonies obviously deserve their own chapter. With great patience, the structure was first built in Japan and then re-built in the residence. Even though its architecture is typical of the country, it has not been influenced by any particular house. It is made of Japanese cedar and divided into two zones: one with the traditional *tatami* (woven-straw floor mat) and another, with benches and tables. With ample windows looking out to the pond, the view is, frankly, captivating.

Near the end of the 12th century, a Buddhist monk – Eisai – brought the custom of the tea ceremony to Japan from China. Later, in the 16th century, another monk – Sen no Rikyu – established the ceremony's spiritual foundation by introducing elements of Zen Buddhism: harmony between people and nature, respect and gratitude towards all things. The actual ceremony – according to experts it can last up to four hours – takes place before the guests, and each element in it makes sense: the architecture of the house, the utensils used, the arrangement of the flowers, the hanging scrolls, the grace of the movements.

Opposite page
An endless corridor overlooking the Japanese-style garden leads from the main building to the ochashitsu. The red rug contributes to the dramatic effect.

Above
The teahouse at the embassy is named "yu-yu-an", which means "relaxed place". It exemplifies traditional Japanese architecture, but is not patterned after any specific teahouse of the past. In fact, the teahouse combines elements of various styles and has both a traditional tatami *(woven straw mat) area, and one with benches and tables characteristic of the* ryurei-*style tea ceremony.*

The modern motif of this salon includes identical cloud-patterned wallpaper and curtains which give the room a contemporary look. The custom-designed chandelier by Minami Tada serves as a ceiling sculpture to complement the décor of the room. A major feature of the room is "Destination", an abstract painting by Japanese artist Toko Shinoda. This room is used primarily for small gatherings during which tea or cocktails may be served.

KUWAIT

The Embassy of the State of Kuwait encompasses both the chancery and the ambassadorial residence. Architecturally, it embraces both the traditional and contemporary aspects of Kuwait. Its modern features evoke the oil boom which started in the 1950s and changed Kuwait from a pearl-diving city-state into a technologically and financially adept modern nation. But visitors are also reminded of Kuwait's immensely rich Arab and Islamic history and heritage.

Completed in 1965 by the American architect Van Fossen Schwab, the Embassy is oblong, a rectangular shape that characterizes the first known mosque, as well as Kuwait's Parliament, which sits along Kuwait City's *corniche* facing the Persian Gulf. The Embassy's notable Arabesque architecture, as well as its intricate interior decorations, reflect and celebrate both the old and new. This was no small challenge for the Baltimore-born architect.

Kuwait is the size of New Jersey, yet it has one of the highest per capita incomes in the world. It boasts of the third largest oil reserves in the world (after Saudi Arabia and Iraq). So not surprisingly, Kuwait enjoys the luxury of having an embassy in Washington that conveys prosperity and opulence. Nevertheless, simplicity of design and articulation of space are the hallmarks of Kuwait's embassy. Clean, bold lines predominate. The embassy's diplomatic mission and ambassadorial residence are connected by a large hall called the *loggia* (or central hall), which is painted in lush blue tones. White stone colonnades, expressing the classic Islamic arch, line the building, while marble graces the exterior. Kuwait's seal is central to the design. It features a picture of a *dhow*, the trading and pearling ship on which Kuwaiti seafarers once plied the Persian Gulf and Indian Ocean. It is also adorned by red, white and Islamic green – Kuwait's national colors.

Schwab said that seven designers decorated the interior. The official chancery history, however, only mentions the involvement of an Italian born in Egypt and a Lebanese. The design unifies two phases of Islamic decorative art: modern Islamic art, represented by the *loggia*, and a medieval Damascene influence, as seen in the Omayyad room. In the *loggia*, Baccarat crystal lamps purchased from an Indian museum illuminate the central hall. Its walls are entirely covered by thirty-seven thousand pieces of hand-carved walnut, enhanced by mirrors, creating an amplified sense of space. The blue and white tiles on the floor are repeated in the graceful water fountain, specially designed for the embassy in Italy. These combined elements provide balance and wholeness, creating a room with the calming powers of an oasis.

Strong in its Islamic essence, the Omayyad room creates the ambiance of a Syrian manor house of three centuries ago. Indeed, its walls belonged to and were transported from a 1755 palace in Damascus. It is furnished with assorted chairs, silk cushions, a finely carved wooden center table, bronze lamps, and other handicrafts that represent different periods of Arab culture. Modern conveniences, such as a swimming pool, have been incorporated into the design and more recently, for security reasons, a guardhouse. Even this "detail" makes sense from a semantic point of view. The name Kuwait originates in the word *kut*, which means fortification.

The loggia, *or great hall, is decorated by Baccarat crystal lamps purchased from a museum in India. The walls are of hand-carved walnut, a mosaic of 37 000 pieces enhanced by mirrors. Blue and white tiles, custom-designed and imported from Italy, line the water fountain basin, and the fountain itself creates a relaxing atmosphere.*

Page 192
Schwab, the architect, designed the exteriors. According to him, up to seven professionals participated in the interior décor. The Chancery's official version speaks of two – an Italian born in Egypt and a Lebanese. It matters little whether there were two or seven, because passing through the diverse rooms, each with a different ambiance, is a pleasant experience.

Right

The room creates the ambiance of a palace in Syria three centuries ago. Its walls were transported from an Omayyad-dynasty palace, built in Damascus in 1755. Nothing is lacking, and nothing is in excess in this rectangular room. There is an abundance but not an overload of fluffy chairs and lively silk cushions, a finely-carved wooden center table and doors covered in leather. Bronze lamps illuminate the space.

LEBANON

The Lebanese are proud of the remarkable features of their country. Lebanon enjoys a privileged Mediterranean climate (300 hundred sunny days per year), an extraordinary cuisine, notable artists and a geography that has been a meeting point for diverse and ancient civilizations. In any conversation, they bring up Kahlil Gibran, the celebrated author of "The Prophet" (translated into more than 25 languages) and the cedar, the native and omnipresent tree that is said to represent the fortitude and perennial nature of the country. It is not an accident that it is remembered time and time again, in poetry, painting, sculpture…and even in the Limoges china pattern that Lebanese embassies use abroad. And, of course, it is the central image on the national flag.

The Government of Lebanon bought the property in 1949 for the residence of its ambassadors in Washington, six years after the country gained its independence from the French mandate. All of the country's most treasured cultural icons are present under the roof of the residence. The reason for choosing this mansion is obvious: it has white stucco, tiles, mosaics and small balconies, in the typical style of the Mediterranean mansion, but enthusiastically reinterpreted by U.S. architects of the nineteen-twenties and thirties. Unique pieces were brought over from the Lebanese homeland. Just inside the wrought iron gates of the property, in the garden, a rarity: a carved stone "Garland Sarcophagus" with Medusa head and swags, dating from the 2nd century.

Light enters the interior of the house in abundance, laying bare the ample staircase in the entrance hall, the holm-oak floors, the marble chimneys, the Persian rugs, the Steinway grand piano and the French porcelains. The just tribute paid to the diverse and famous Lebanese artists of the past century, who are an important part of the life of the nation, is notable. Lebanon's collective memory is found on the walls of the drawing room, music room and family dining room. There are reproductions of the art of Kahlil Gibran, impressive watercolors and a magnificent collection of his nudes. Other rooms are decorated with landscapes by Omar Onsi and Cesar Gemayel, and with the increasingly more abstract paintings of Saliba Douaihy, famous for his frescoes in the Maronite Church of Diman, Lebanon.

The walls of the drawing room are covered in silk damask and decorated with varied landscapes by famous Lebanese artists, such as Saliba Douaihy, Omar Onsi and Cesar Gemayel. Four chandeliers flood the room with light. The furniture is French, and Persian rugs in vibrant colors cover the oak floor.

Opposite page
The grand staircase and carved balustrade capture the spotlight in the entrance hall. The marble fountain, with three cherubs, graces the foyer.

Above
Tables set for dinner for sixty guests. The dining room is illuminated by a great crystal chandelier. The floors are parquet and the walls are wood-paneled.

MEXICO

The Mexican Cultural Institute

Franklin MacVeagh was a lucky man. And talented, too. He hailed from Pennsylvania and when the time came to go to college, he was accepted to Yale; after college, he wanted to go on to study law and Columbia Law School opened its doors to him. But the desire to practice did not last too long. A short time after working in Philadelphia, he decided he had neither the money nor the health to continue and left for Chicago. There, he joined a grocery business. When he began to see the light at the end of the tunnel, the establishment burned down. This was MacVeagh's opportunity to set out on his own and become one of the largest wholesalers in the country.

But he was not just an able businessman. He was also a Director of the Commercial National Bank of Chicago for 28 years; he was a founder of and/or belonged to an endless list of civic organizations, charity institutions and historical and artistic academies. But he was a real *aficionado* of architecture. And he pursued his hobby in his free time when he moved to Washington to become President Taft's Secretary of the Treasury. He and his wife Emily rented the Pink Palace, as it was called, built by Totten on exclusive 16th Street. But the property he had an eye on, the one he really liked, was being built a block away from his home: number 2829 on 16th Street. He had discovered it during one of his habitual excursions and he fell in love with it because it embodied everything that signified "good taste" for him. The only mystery was, who owned it? Mary Foote Henderson, who had the best lots in the neighborhood, had sold the land in 1909; Nathan Wyeth, the architect of the West Wing of the White House and the current residences of the embassies of Russia and Chile, among others, had designed it; and the builder was George Fuller. But the name of the property owner remained one of the few well-kept secrets of Washington.

The last time that the MacVeaghs visited the house was on December 24, 1910. By then it was totally furnished and workmen were putting on the final touches. Sick and tired of hearing her husband sing the praises of the refinements of the owner, Emily MacVeagh, who had commissioned the construction, turned around and asked Mr. Secretary if he would like it as a Christmas present.

They inaugurated the house with a party for Helen Taft, the daughter of the President, who attended with the First Lady. But their happiness did not last long. Emily passed away in 1916 after a long illness and MacVeagh returned to Chicago, because he could not bear the house without her. He rented the mansion for five years to the government of the United States, which used it as a guest house for illustrious visitors. Among the distinguished guests who were lodged there were King Albert and Queen Elizabeth of Belgium.

In 1921, during the post-revolutionary government of Álvaro Obregón, Mexico purchased the property, along with a great deal of the furniture, paintings and tapestries, for the residence of its representatives in Washington. An exception was made for the furnishings of the celebrated "Golden Room", which MacVeagh kept for himself and his son. During the closing, he requested that no great changes be made to the house until

The painting of the murals was the first drastic change that the Mexican government introduced into the former MacVeagh mansion. These depict the daily life and history of the country. They also lead us to the French rooms on the second floor and the British library on the third. In these spaces the original décor was wisely retained.

Opposite page and right
*Cultural integration starts
at the entrance hall. We
begin at the colonial altar
(not seen in the photograph)
and continue with the murals
painted by Cueva del Río,
a disciple of Diego Rivera,
which spread over all three
floors. The tension between
the murals and the English
oak staircase is reason
enough to warrant a visit
to this residence.*

after his death. Despite the fact that he lived to the age of 97 (he died in 1934), a few were made. For example, a portico was added to the Italianate façade; the chancery went up on the southern part of the property; and a garage was built.

The mansion's great transformation took place in 1933, when the artist Roberto Cueva del Río, a disciple of Diego Rivera, painted the six inmense murals that run parallel to the awesome staircase. These speak to us, in full color, of the "true Mexico" and describe scenes of daily life and the history of the country. They lead us to the French rooms of the second floor and to the fascinating English library on the third. In these rooms, and wisely, the original decór has remained intact. "Mexico" reappears in full force in the greenhouse next to the dining room. This interior

courtyard, designed by the same Cueva del Río, is literally covered in Talavera tile made in the Mexican city of Puebla. The location is the perfect setting for speeches and performances by popular singers and contemporary dancers. In this same way, the luxurious Music Room, with its wonderful acoustics, is exclusively used for song recitals and concerts. Book launches and the Mexican history series find their natural home in the library.

All of these events now take place in this building, because since 1990, when the Mexican ambassadors moved to another residence, the MacVeagh Palace, born under a lucky star, has been the Mexican Cultural Institute.

The Music Room has always been considered the most luxurious space in this residence. It was modelled after the Music Room at Fontainebleau Castle.
The curved panels, hand-painted in the French style, give this room a perfect resonance. Its acoustics are ideal for individual recitals by tenors or sopranos, or for the series of concerts that are continually held at the Mexican Cultural Institute.

MOROCCO

Our visit to the house began with a good glass of mint tea, the national drink *par excellence*. That is, the tour started the instant we took the first sip. The beauty of the objects set out for the drink on the carpet of the Moroccan Room merits a detailed explanation of its own.

Neither a special time nor reason is needed to drink it. Any time is good and any motive valid. One must always be ready to offer it. And they are always ready in the residence of the representatives of this kingdom in northwest Africa. The imposing samovar used to heat the water is on one side of the room and a series of silver serving trays are placed at the feet of the banquettes that line the walls of the space. One tray is used for the silver boxes that contain the green tea, the fresh mint and the sugar; another to hold the silver teapots (*barrad*) and the glasses used to serve the drink; on yet another lies the dispenser for the orange-flower water used on special occasions; and finally, there is one for the incense holder (*M'Bakhra*), where precious woods of exotic aromas are burned to perfume the space.

A series of carved wooden tables are scattered throughout the diverse spaces of the room, reminding us that the work in wood is a tradition unique to Morocco among the Islamic states of Africa. Among some of the most ornate examples are doors, screens, chests, tea tables and lecterns to rest the Koran on.

The multipurpose uses of this Moroccan Salon are truly surprising. The space can become the warmest of dining rooms in a matter of seconds. A round table is placed against a corner where the banquettes join together, four chairs are brought over and pretty soon you have eight diners seated (four on the banquettes themselves), in an atmosphere of unsurpassable intimacy. The sea of cushions that decorate the room and the Moroccan carpet contribute to this atmosphere. We immediately wonder whether the carpet, being Moroccan and hand-woven, might contain what is called *barake*, that is, beneficial psychic powers.

The other great room of the house is decorated in the European fashion. The great miracle of the kingdom of Morocco is that it has been home to so many peoples – Berbers, Arabs, French, English, Spanish, among many others – and still preserves its own individuality. It is for this reason that the residence of Clewerwall Drive, which was built in 1979 and bought by the Moroccan government from the developer Michael Nash in 1998, is never afraid of contrasts. So it is that this room features a work by the American artist Hilda Thorpe, a painter, sculptor and devotée of Moroccan landscapes and culture. It depicts two women wearing the typical clothing and hats of the Rif Mountain area, a region in the north of the country.

The sunroom repeats the style of decorating, where European antiques and Arab marquetry tables meld in great harmony with one another. A painting by the well-known Moroccan artist Hassan El Glaoui, famous for his brilliant colors and freedom of movement, hangs on the wall. *Fantasia* shows a spectacle where tribes or families compete on

This room features an abundance of European antiques. The painting on the wall depicts two women wearing traditional clothes and hats typical of the Rif Mountain area in the north of Morocco. The artist is Hilda Thorpe, who is devoted to the landscape and culture of Morocco.

Above

The multipurpose uses of this Moroccan Salon are truly surprising. The space can become the warmest of dining rooms in a matter of seconds. The napkins are hand-embroidered in traditional motifs in the city of Fez. In the center, the great silver tray or Al Meeda encloses the sweetest and most delicious of surprises: the celebrated Moroccan pastries, pastilla.

Right

The Moroccan Salon features banquettes that are upholstered in rich fabrics and a multitude of cushions in the traditional Moroccan style. The small wooden thuya *tables are carved by hand. On the right sits a tall samovar used to heat water for the preparation of Moroccan mint tea.*

Left
The decorating style, which combines European antiques with traditional Arab tables that have a marquetry of precious woods, is repeated here. A painting by the Moroccan artist Hassan El Glaoui, famous for his brilliant colors and freedom of movement, occupies a privileged place.

Opposite page
Each and every visitor finds his or her own magnetic pole in the main hall. Some of them find memorable the wrought-iron spiral staircase, while others prefer the T'Bak, the silver platters in pointed shapes that are used to carry freshly-baked bread to the table, set on one side of the room.

horseback in front of a huge audience. A large part of the painter's work is inspired by this event.

Each and every visitor finds his or her own magnetic pole in the main hall. Some of them find memorable the wrought-iron spiral staircase, while others prefer the *T'Bak,* silver platters in pointed shapes that are used to carry freshly-baked bread to the tables that are set on one side of the room. They are as pretty and as inspiring as the *Al Meeda,* those other marvels of engraved silver that open to show a sweet revelation: their interior holds a wide range of delicate and tempting Moroccan delicacies, or *pastilla,* waiting to disappear into the mouths of visitors.

NORWAY

In 1905 Norway and Sweden dissolved the union that had tied the two countries together since 1814, and Norway established its own Foreign Service. The first nomination to be announced was the envoy to the United States of America, Minister Christian Hauge. With his own money (and his wife's!) he soon started constructing what he planned to be the Norwegian Legation building at the corner of 24th Street and Massachusetts Avenue, but he died suddenly in 1907, before he could move in. The mansion today is the Cameroon Embassy.

In 1930, after much discussion, the Norwegian government bought a plot a bit higher up Massachusetts Avenue, at the corner of 34th Street, to build a combined chancery and residence. When the doors of that mansion finally opened in April 1931, all involved breathed a sigh of relief. After long years, the Norwegian delegation finally had their own diplomatic home. It was in a privileged area, known as Massachusetts Avenue Park, described in a sales brochure of the time as "without a doubt the most beautiful area in the most beautiful city in the world."

The Norwegian government had signed a contract the year before with the well-known construction company Sibour, which had already done work for the embassies of Spain and Argentina, among others. The architect John Whelan designed the house in what is known as the English Renaissance style, which was very popular at the time in all its American versions.

The Massachusetts Avenue building was soon fully inhabited, and how! In accordance with the instructions of the client, it had a total of 23 rooms. The exterior was ornamental limestone, the roof was hand-crafted tile. The first floor of the three-story building housed six chancery offices, a smoking room, a file room and quarters for the domestic staff. The mansion orginally had a separate office entrance, but it was later sealed. The second floor contained the reception salons and the third floor, bedrooms and guest rooms.

During World War II the embassy staff increased and an annex was built in 1941 to house 12 offices. The new wing was decorated with murals from the Norwegian Pavilion at the New York World's Fair of 1939, depicting the classical legends and motifs of the country. It was officially inaugurated by the Norwegian Crown Princess Märtha, who lived in Washington D.C. with her children during the war.

But even that space soon became too small, and two other houses in the neighborhood were acquired. In 1978 the annex wing and the neighboring residence were demolished to make room for a new chancery. The materials were chosen with such care that they are in perfect harmony with the old mansion. The two buildings are interconnected by a colonnade leading to the garden. An old, rather narrow, hallway was excavated and replaced by a heated pool. The spouse of the present ambassador, Ellen Sofie Vollebaek, says that "we have our own Norwegian Channel."

An almost life-size portrait of Norway's first post-union King, Haakon VII, hangs in the elegant and illuminated foyer. You reach the second floor by a wide spiral staircase. A bust of his young son, who later became King Olav V, sits on a shelf on the way up. The library is

The walls of the library still have the original Norwegian-spruce panelling, with built-in book-shelves. Over the fireplace a woodcut by Edvard Munch, "Man's Head in Woman's Hair." "Summer", the painting on the back wall, is by Norwegian artist Hugo Lous Mohr (1889-1970).

Left
To the left of the fireplace:
"Shellback", by Norwegian
painter Christian Krogh
(1852-1925). To the right of
the fireplace: a lithograph by
Edvard Munch: "Jealousy II".

Above
Portrait of King Haakon VII,
by Brynjulf Strandenaes, a
Norwegian painter who
immigrated to the U.S.
Haakon, born as Prince
Carl of Denmark, became
Norway's first king after
the union with Sweden
ended in 1905.

very comfortable and there is a privileged space for two paintings by the American-born artist William H. Singer, who spent all his summers in Norway from 1910 till his death.

One of the corners of the drawing room is taken up by a grand piano and original Norwegian furniture. Paintings, some of them on loan from Norway's National Gallery of Art, line the walls. Landscapes predominate in the painting collection here. At one end sits an imposing Biedermeier sofa. An enormous rug, a present from the Russian government many years ago, covers the middle of the chamber. Classic blue-and-white porcelain sits on a table. On the walls of the dining room, in a very different mood and setting, hang works by the great Norwegian painter Edvard Munch. The effect is all…very royal.

PANAMA

If, on the day you visit this embassy residence, you are feeling particularly imaginative and full of nationalistic spirit, you will fully appreciate the choice Ambassador Ernesto Jaén De la Guardia made in 1942. You might even think that one of the reasons he chose this particular house is the double staircase leading to the front door, which alludes, even if very indirectly, to his country's privileged geographical position. If you choose to ascend by the left steps you enter by the Pacific Ocean, and if you choose the right steps, you enter by the Atlantic. But finally, both flow into the same channel: a path surrounded by plants and trees signaling Washington's springtime. Along with rhododendrons, there are azaleas, Japanese maples and dogwoods.

And even if the staircase failed to make you feel that you were in Panama, the country's idiosyncrasies are present in the vestibule. Eclecticism reigns. This is, after all, the bridge country. For centuries, people, merchandise and ideas, all coming from the most diverse regions of the world, have moved through the isthmus. So, not surprisingly, what we at first thought was an alarm that rang every time we got near the entrance's Coromandel screen turned out to be a stentorian grandfather clock ringing at full volume.

The mix of East and West is everywhere, throughout the length and breadth of the house. It peaks in the principal salon. There, between French chests of drawers, English tables and Chinese vases, sits an Italian *secrétaire*. It doesn't intrude on the other pieces and it is not intruded upon. And this is, in essence, the house's great charm. Thanks to the clever placement of modern and antique pieces, and Panamanian and imported objects, everything coexists harmoniously. Indeed, if there one word that best describes the house, it is cozy. Without having the large scale or pretentiousness of the American-style palaces that are used by certain diplomatic missions, this house is of ample size. It was built on a human scale, in an exclusive neighborhood, by a wealthy American couple who decided, in 1929, to create their dream residence on earth. It has fine finishings throughout, a yard, a terrace and a swimming pool.

Light abounds, as it does in the isthmus. It filters through the high "cathedral" windows that line the staircase as well as those that face the pool patio. Whatever light remains is appropriated by the sunny sitting room that is next to the living room, appropriately called the "Florida" room, and unanimously preferred by both guests and hosts. On the original stonewall hangs a painting by the well-known Panamanian painter and architect, Guillermo Trujillo. He is a passionate scholar of the work of the Kuna Indians. It is to that tribe of the San Blas Islands that we owe the intricate and colorful *Molas*. *Molas* are textiles made from pieces of cloth superimposed on other pieces. The magic of the colors and the intricacy of the work lift them far above their humble origins.

The library adds to this study in contrasts. The muted tones of the collection of Pre-Columbian ceramics blend seamlessly with the dark wood-paneling on the walls. The fearless colors of "The Dance", a painting by the artist Olga Sinclair that is as Panamanian as the funerary vases, provide the counterpoint.

Without having the scale or pretentiousness of the American-style palaces that lodge certain diplomatic missions, this house is of ample size. It was built on a human scale, in an exclusive neighborhood, by a wealthy American couple who decided, in 1929, to build their dream residence on earth. It has fine finishings throughout, a yard, a terrace and a swimming pool.

Left

*Mirrors line the parts of
the wall that not covered
by silk wallpaper. In the
background, we can see
two of the three works by
Panamanian painter Roberto
Lewis, considered the father
of Panamanian art.
Ambassador Ernesto Jaén
De la Guardia commissioned
them shortly after he
acquired the new site.*

Above

*The mix of East and West is
found throughout the length
and breadth of the house.
It peaks in the principal salon.
The house's great charm is
in the clever placement of
modern and antique pieces
and Panamanian and
imported objects. They all
coexist in perfect harmony.
The house is best described
as "cozy."*

In the dining room, on the afternoon that we visited the residence, the competition for our attention was fierce. The only things more wonderful than the Reed and Barton silver, Royal Worcester china, huge hammered-silver soup tureen and the two paintings by the father of Panamanian art, Roberto Lewis, were the aromas emanating from the kitchen. All the clocks rang cocktail time. And rum, in the tropics, always tastes better when accompanied by *empanadas*.

PERU

The Peruvian government showed the same meticulous attention to detail in choosing and furnishing the residence of its ambassadors in Washington as Charles H. Tompkins and his wife Lida did when they selected the site for their new mansion on a wooded hill in the Rock Creek Park area.

Tompkins was one of the leaders of the development of the capital – among the projects that his company built were the East and West Executive Offices of the White House and the Reflecting Pool in the Lincoln Memorial – and he knew like no one else the historical value of the land he chose to build his home on in 1928. Apart from its obvious beauty and exclusive location, it had been the site, one hundred and forty years ago, of Battery Terrill, an unarmed auxiliary fort used to defend Washington during the Civil War.

But this wasn't the only concern of the new owners. They chose as its architect the prestigious Horace Peaslee, who had designed many federal and municipal buildings and private houses. He had also designed Meridian Hill Park and restored such houses as Dumbarton Oaks and the Bowie Sevier in Georgetown. After spending three years studying residences in Delaware and Virginia, the owners decided upon late-Georgian architecture for the style of their own house. The Garrison Street mansion is a good example of the renaissance of American colonial architecture. The polished and burnt stone from the historic Peirce Mill of Rock Creek – which dates back to 1820 – inspired Tompkins' design of the façade. What no one ever imagined was that this mansion would become a privileged showcase for the ancient culture of Peru, starting in 1944, when the Peruvian government bought the house.

These days, diplomats come and go. Some contribute personal belongings that have been famous in the Washington of their time – like the collection of Taurine art belonging to Ambassador Fernando Berckmeyer or the fabulous collection of colonial art of Ambassador Celso Pastor – but the house's three floors and sixteen rooms are never left empty. The mansion's pre-Columbian ceramics from the Moche, Chimu, Nazca cultures; the colonial paintings from the Cuzco and Lima schools; the objects in hammered silver; the costumbrista watercolors, which describe the customs of the country in the style of Pancho Fierro; and the Pucaran bulls – all remain, always waiting for new inhabitants. These pieces are the property of the government.

The dining room table has been the best witness of Peru's unmatchable cuisine, from classic cebiches to tiraditos. More recent has been the appearance of the fragile and indescribable alfajores, the dessert treats that Julia, the wife of ambassador Allan Wagner, assembled at dawn. And what to say of the pisco sours enjoyed in the garden, near the statue of the Huitoto child by Felipe Lettersten? Or of the image of the Virgin that is neither image nor Virgin, but was carved by the will of water in a niche beyond the pool? Or about the "open forest" path that goes all the way from the imposing iron gate to the entrance of the house? What we didn't see, although they are surely there, were the deer, those persona non grata which abound in Washington's gardens.

"Virgin with Sword" (Saint Catherine of Alexandria), Colonial painting of the Cuzco school.

Above
Oak staircase that leads to the private quarters. On the landing, an oil painting by the contemporary Peruvian painter Pedro Caballero. In the oval entrance hall, over the wooden chest of drawers, a colonial painting from the Cuzco school, "The Adoration of the Three Kings".

Right
In the spacious drawing room, the centers of attention are the Colonial paintings of the school of Cuzco, "Defense of the Eucharist", "Virgin with Child", and "The Visitation". But there's more…above the chimney and making its presence known, a fragment of an altarpiece in wood and gold leaf.

Above

This dining room table has been a faithful witness to the unmatchable cuisine of Peru, from classic cebiches, to tiraditos and alfajores. On the table, a soup tureen and a pair of fighting cocks by Camusso in hammered silver, which belong to ambassador's Wagner collection, are traditional works from the renowned Peruvian silversmithing tradition. At one end, the breakfast room, where an ancient carved wooden wardrobe stands out. On top of it, pure national artistry: the Qonopa or little bulls of Pucará.

Below

The most characteristic feature of the music room is its roof with exposed rafters. In the center, oil paintings: "Great Priest" by Armando Villegas, "Street Scene, Lima" by F. Stratton, and "Plaza de Acho" by M. Aldana.

Upon this chest of drawers in the library, and of noteworthy beauty, is the "Mamacha", or "Virgen de la Leche" by Hilario Mendivil, one of the most famous Cuzco-born painters of religious images, whose work is characterized by the long necks of his figures. On the left an excellent oil painting by the Peruvian artist Antonio Maro (both works belong to the Wagners's personal collection). At one end, the Watercolor Room, where a collection of watercolors presents a detailed introduction to the customs and costumes of Peruvian society in the era of the Viceroys and the beginnings of the Republic.

And what to say of the pisco sours enjoyed in the garden, near the statue of the Huitoto child by Felipe Lettersten? Or of the image of the Virgin that is neither image nor Virgin, but was carved by the will of water in a niche beyond the pool?

PORTUGAL

During one of his trips to Washington to visit his sisters – Annie, a widow, and Mary, who was single – painting magnate W. Lawrence concluded that it was not really fair that they had to live in a rented house, while he was so wealthy. He decided to build them a house in the very neighborhood where they lived. His good instincts told him that land in Washington which was cheap in 1908, would be worth millions later. And so it happened that what was originally going to be one home on the heights of Kalorama became two. The Lawrence sisters lived in the first one until 1916. They decided to sell it after their brother died. It is now the residence of the French ambassadors.

The second property, built for investment purposes in 1914, was, like the first one, the work of the famous New York architect, Jules Henri de Sibour. It was purchased by the Portuguese government in 1946. The first task, once it became Portugal's, was to make it "Portuguese." The architect Frederick Brooks was commissioned to oversee the expansion and renovation; but not the interior design. Leonardo Castro Freire, a Portuguese native, took charge of the décor. Apart from having a grand house, the new owners wanted to feel at home in the space and make their guests feel the same. And no traditional Portuguese home does without tiles, rugs and hand-made china. When there is enough money, the floors are marble. And when there is lineage, the coat of arms is always welcome.

The Kalorama residence has all this and more. The name means "Good View", and the privileged location certainly contributed to it. The country's shield presides over the entrance. A vestibule with Estremoz marble floors was added and the celebrated glazed tiles make their appearance on the walls of the staircase that leads to the second floor. The dining room, that most Portuguese of rooms, takes all honors when it comes to tiles. There is marble in the fountain and tile on the bottom third of the walls. Glazed tiles or *azulejos*, however you wish to call them, speak to us of the hundreds of years of history that the industry has in the country. It is said that no one competes with Portugal in this field, either in quantity or quality. The first designs, now left behind, came from the Moorish tradition,– for it was the Moors who introduced tiles in the 14th century, when the only designs allowed were geometric ones. The monopoly of certain colors and tones, a result of the wares navigators brought back from their exploration of the oceans, no longer applies. When Oriental ceramics were covered in blue and white, for example, so were Portuguese tiles. Things reached a point where it was thought that the name *azulejo* derived from the color *azul*, (blue in Portuguese) and not from the Arabic *al zulaic*, which was its true origin.

The truth is that polychromy has a long tradition. History tells us that after the earthquake of 1755, Lisbon wanted to forget the disaster and rebuild in colors. The result was that tiles of every tone and design were used in the exteriors and interiors of buildings, both public and private, and in rooms grand and small, from bathrooms to dining halls. Another incentive was that the Portuguese had already discovered, from their colony in Brazil, that tiles were an effective barrier against humidity.

One of the decorating principles was to give the residence the atmosphere of 18th century Portugal, as a homage to an era of artistic rebirth in the country.

Above

In the Map Room, in the company of objects much loved by the Portuguese, like the flower vases from Vista Alegre and the roosters from the Royal Rato Factory in Lisbon, one comes upon the invaluable collection of 17th and 18th century maps which give the room its name. Over the chimney hangs a painting by Joseph Noel depicting the Battle of Cape San Vicente (in the south of Portugal), the historic clash between the Spanish navy and the British fleet led by Lord Nelson.

Right

A work by the painter Charles Antoine Coypel (1694-1754) hangs over the chimney, accompanied by "rose family" porcelain plates. A hand-woven Arraiolos rug of incalculable value covers the floor of the Great Reception Hall.

Castro Freire, the decorator, chose Estremoz marble for the floors of the entrance hall and the staircase. Portugal has great deposits of this stone. The walls are decorated with polychrome mosaics, in the style of the 18th century churches of Coimbra.

But tile-making was not the only craft at which Portugal excelled. Take the dining room, for example: the great hand-woven Arraiolos rug that covers the floors is as impressive as any mosaic. When did this technique arrive in the Iberian Peninsula? The exact date is unknown, but some think that it was in the 13th century. Another Arraiolos, just as valuable, covers the floor of the great reception hall or Yellow Salon; there it competes, stitch by stitch, with the 18th century Arras tapestry, *Verdure*, which covers the walls, and with the marvelous 18th century Dutch *armoire* in the back. The *armoire*, now transformed into a display case, exhibits some valuable porcelain pieces "of the kind brought over by The India

The dining room – it has been said – is the most Portuguese of rooms. The materials all hail from Portugal: the marble of the fountain, the glazed wall tiles, the silverware on the table, and the marvelous hand-woven Arraiolos rug that covers the floor. The leather seats and the rosewood furniture were specially brought over from the Ricardo do Espírito Santo Silva Museum-School for Decorative Arts.

Company during the 17th and 18th centuries," explains Ana da Rocha París, the ambassador's wife and owner of the collection. She goes on to point out that they belong to "the rose family, the green family and the blue and white one."

Adjoining the Yellow Salon, there is a smaller room, full of objects much loved by the Portuguese – like the flower vases from Vista Alegre and the roosters from the Royal Rato Factory in Lisbon. There, one sees an invaluable collection of 17th and 18th century maps. How could they be absent from the official residence of the country of navigators?

ROMANIA

Until 1994 the chancery and the ambassador's residence shared a house. And what a house it was! It was a splendid *Beaux-Arts* mansion constructed in 1907 on the corner of 23rd Street and Sheridan Circle by Carrere and Hastings. This was the same team that designed the Cosmos Club in Washington and the Frick Residence in New York. Romania bought the house in 1921.

But ambassadors don't live here anymore. For the past eight years their residence has been a 30th Street mansion, rented from the State Department. Strategically located, much like Romania on the map of Europe, its neighbors include, among others, the house of the Vice-President of the United States as well as the chanceries of Brazil, Turkey, Italy and Japan. Built by a French architect, the Romanian miracle comes alive in the words of the young and gracious wife of the ambassador, Carmen Ducaru, who from the very start says that the residence is "a traditional Romanian house in its interior design and decoration."

According to her, there is no Romanian house lacking icons, pottery and rugs. What is less common, however, is that between the chancery and the residence there are more than 30 sculptures by the renowned artist Marcel Guguianu – a disciple of the famous Romanian sculptor Constantin Brancusi. It is a national characteristic to mix form and function, and many of their everyday objects, in large part hand-crafted, are pieces that art collectors would pay dearly to own. A good example of such pieces is the hand-painted furniture from Transylvania.

From the first floor of smaller proportions – very common in homes built in the thirties- the staircase leads to the huge salons of the second floor and then continues its march towards the private quarters of the third story. A collection of *naïve* paintings, done by Romanian children, hangs all along the staircase and emphasizes two things that are at the very heart of the Romanian soul: harmony and spirituality.

In the public areas, the rugs of the principal drawing room and dining room speak, in turn, of the centuries-long weaving and embroidery traditions of Romania. But differences exist, too: the rugs from Moldavia are distinguished by their geometric motifs, the Oltenian ones by their floral patterns, and those from the Maramures region by their anthropomorphic elements.

The drawing room shelves are proof positive that this residence is Romanian to the core. Orthodox icons – in wood and glass – from the personal collection of the ambassadors share the room, the space and the spotlight with marble and bronze sculptures, ceramic dishes and pitchers. When it comes to icons, Romania, along with Russia and Greece, has much to offer the world. The icon's great artistic apogee came during the 17th and 18th centuries, when centers dedicated to the painting of images on wood, in which the sacred and the worldly stand in natural harmony, proliferated throughout the country.

Pottery has a millennial tradition in Romania. It has played a key role in traditional interior decoration, and museums exhibit valuable items dating back to the Neolithic period. Over the centuries, there have been different uses, variations and classifications of

The drawing room shelves are proof positive that this residence is Romanian to the core. Wood and glass Orthodox icons from the personal collection of the ambassadors share the room, the space and the spotlight with marble and bronze sculptures, ceramic dishes and pitchers.

Pottery has a millennial tradition in Romania. It has played a key role in traditional interior decoration, and museums exhibit valuable items dating back to the Neolithic period. Over the centuries, there have been different uses, variations and classifications of the earthenware; the most famous center for pottery is in Horezu. And porcelain pieces from the Curtea de Arges workshop are true works of art.

the earthenware; the most famous center for pottery is in Horezu. The porcelain pieces from the Curtea de Arges workshop are true works of art.

Nevertheless, what is most admirable about the Romanians – who have endured innumerable invasions since the time of the Romans – is their fidelity to their language, their religion and their customs. To what or whom can we attribute this miracle? Maybe the explanation is to be found in the Carpathian Mountains, the blue Danube and the Black Sea.

In the great public area, the rugs of the principal drawing room and dining room speak, in turn, of the centuries-long tradition of weaving and embroidery in Romania. But differences exist, too: the rugs from Moldavia are distinguished by their geometric motifs, the Oltenian ones by the floral patterns, and those from the Maramures region by their anthropomorphic elements.

RUSSIA

Hattie Sanger Pullman was not your typical mother-in-law. For starters, she was fascinated by the political career of her son-in-law, Frank O. Lowden, elected and re-elected to Congress from Illinois. The multimillionaire mother-in-law, the widow of the sleeping-car magnate George Pullman, decided that since Lowden and his daughter were going to stay in the capital for a long time, it would be a good thing for them to have a house of their own. But it couldn't be just any dwelling, because if her son-in-law's political career continued on its lightning path, it might even land him in the White House.

With those criteria in mind, the obvious choice for the building's architect was Nathan Wyeth, who, at that very time, was in charge of the expansion of the West Wing offices of the White House.

The mansion was one of the most costly buildings to go up in turn-of-the-century Washington. It was built to Hattie's exact specifications and aspirations: an imposing structure, extensive reception salons, and fine finishes throughout.

Because of its mixture of styles and lack of originality, there is still debate about whether the Pullman mansion represents the pinnacle of Wyeth's achievements or his gravest mortal sin. But this residence, with all that its walls have seen and heard, is now a fundamental cornerstone of Washington history.

But the Pullmans never danced in the so-very-Versailles Golden Salon or dined in the immense, formal, oak-lined dining room. Their son-in-law fell ill, could not run for re-election and consequently never returned to the capital. From then on, his mother-in-law lost all interest in the property and put it on the market, furnishings and all. But it was not easy to unload such a place at such a price and in such times. In the end, her good friend Nathalie Hays Hammond, the wife of the millionaire mining engineer who would later buy the current French embassy, bought it from her. A few months later, Hammond sold the mansion to the government of the Russian Czar for $ 350 000.

It has always been said that no one greeted Nicholas II's purchase with more applause than the Russian Ambassador Georgi Bakhmeteff and his wife, the aristocratic and talented Marie Beale, an American woman who loved to live in the grand manner. From 1914 onwards, the 64-room dwelling was run as another imperial palace by the diplomatic couple, with the help of their French chef, his 12 assistants and the other 40 people that made up its staff of servants. It was then that the whole city discovered how one entertained in czarist Russia.

In 1917, naturally, the party stopped. The Czar abdicated, and Kerenski's provisional government gave notice that its new representative, Boris Bakhmeteff, would arrive in Washington within the same week. The new envoy had nothing in common with his predecessor, apart from the shared last name, a detail that the latter made sure was spread *urbi et orbi*, when he was not calling his successor a master plumber.

Immediately afterwards, the czarist ambassador and his wife decamped to live in France. But first they dismantled the 16th street embassy and took with them all of its valuable

In the spectacular Gold Salon all that shines is… laminated gold. When Eugene Schoen, the famous New York architect and designer, was asked to modernize the Embassy, he categorically insisted on a respect for the original décor, down to the last curlicue on the most diminutive cupid. The multiplying of the chandeliers by the mirrors was a much-utilized effect in the mansions of the era.

belongings, on the theory that neither its Louis XV and XVI sofas, nor its valuable chairs, tables and rugs belonged to the "provisional government." Besides, they most certainly needed them to furnish the house they were planning to build in Paris, which was to be, as far as possible, an exact replica of the Pullman mansion, with Wyeth as its architect. The house never became a reality, but the new ambassador was too busy going back and forth to the State Department to care about the missing furnishings, and he adorned the house with the first set of non-pretentious furniture he found.

When the great socialist revolution occurred in October and the United States decided not to recognize the new regime, the embassy entered into a period of lethargy that lasted for over ten years. Bakhmeteff left for New York to teach engineering at Columbia University and the walls and furniture of the embassy were covered with cheap drop-cloths.

Everything changed with Franklin Delano Roosevelt's election as president. When he recognized the Soviet Union in 1933, preparations began to receive a new ambassador. The initial idea was to modernize the whole house, starting with the kitchen and the bathrooms. Eugene Schoen, a prestigious New York architect, was hired to undertake the work. But the minute Mr. Schoen entered the mansion and saw the state its coffered interiors were in, he thought that it would be easier and cheaper to buy a new mansion than to restore the old one. He nevertheless dedicated himself to renovating the kitchen and the fourteen bathrooms, announcing that he would not touch even a hair of the most insignificant cupids that decorated the mansion. Thanks to the antique imperial Russian furnishings that were brought in, additional pieces bought from Edith Rockefeller McCormick and Schoen's deft work, the house resumed its old palatial airs and was ready to receive the new ambassador, Alexander Troyanovsky.

Barely four months had elapsed since Troyanosvsky's arrival and the crowning of the residence with the hammer and sickle, when he amazed the notables of Washington by throwing the party of the year. Not all succeeding ambassadors were like the Troyanovskys. Nevertheless, with some representatives more dour than others, the grand reception celebrating the October revolution continued at the residence for many decades, with a vary-

Above
The Gold Salon or Concert hall has been the principal setting for the grand receptions in this Embassy.

Opposite page
For a long time the first floor housed offices for embassy personnel. These later became reception salons, somewhat less informal than those of the second floor.

ing stream of personalities whose presence depended on the degree of tension in the relations between the Soviet Union and the United States.

The residence maintained its same aspect with relatively few changes, especially the portraits of Soviet leaders exhibited in the painting gallery, until Khrushchev's visit in 1959, which was the opportunity for another important renovation. It was also then that President Eisenhower first set foot in this embassy, for the reception in his honor given by the Soviet leader.

The sixties were marked by the efficiency, style and elegance of Ambassador Anatoly Dobrynin, while the Cold War period saw an anti-aesthetic row of antennae appear on the roof of the mansion. After that came *glasnost, perestroika* and the dismemberment of the Soviet Union. At the very end of 1991, the Russian tri-color flag was raised on the ex-Pullman mansion, signifying the birth of the New Russia, the one we now know.

Opposite page
This unusual small parlor, located at one end of the dining room, was heavily curtained at one time.

Right
Painting by well-known Russian artists of different eras decorate the walls, including such well-known names as: I. Aivazovsky, M. Nesterov, K. Makovsky, A. Savrasov, F. Sychkov.

Its current tenants – Ambassador Yuri Ushakov and his dynamic wife Svetlana – were the driving force behind an ambitious restoration project that brought back the grandeur of the Pullman house. As a result of this enormous endeavor, entirely undertaken by Russian craftsmen, the plain offices with linoleum floors and boarded-up fireplaces that had dominated the building for decades were turned into reception salons and given an appearance as close as possible to the original ones. Nowadays the Russian Ambassador's residence is a familiar site among Washingtonians, the diplomatic corps and the Russian community, not only for its grand receptions but also for its art exhibitions, musical recitals and other cultural events.

Svetlana Ushakov summarized it well : "this house has history and it lives."

SINGAPORE

This is a good residence in a grand neighborhood with a great view of Rock Creek Park. Built in 1990, it is relatively new and not too large. The government of Singapore, which had been looking for a new residence, purchased it, exchanging a modern glass house with a view of the woods for a handsome brick house at the edge of a park.

There is no history here of a rich widow selling the small palace to her son for $20 dollars, as happened with Brazil's embassy, or of the millionaire couple that had to sell the mansion after the Crash of the 1930s, as happened with many other mansions in the city.

A renowned architect isn't the main point either. Nevertheless, he deserves praise. The residence is modern Georgian and the solution given to the garage is very clever indeed. Placed next to the house, it was sunk to an underground level and thus unsightly vehicles do not mar the landscape, leaving the center stage, at least in springtime, to the cherry blossoms on the terrace.

The magic begins upon entering. It starts with the light that pours into the hall from the large staircase windows. It gathers steam when one comes upon the unexpected detail of the mother-of-pearl Nautilus shells placed on the rise of the first steps. The greenery that presides over the vestibule contributes to the magical effect. We are now in Singapore, the Garden City, and in Singapore the air is scented by palm trees.

On the right, we come into the principal salon. It is all done in formal white. There are white walls, white furnishings and white orchids, a neutral décor that welcomes the personal *objets* of the diplomat in residence. The large, Regency-style marble chimney, however, is less discreet. But it is balanced by the subtle charm of a set of small Shona stone sculptures from Zimbabwe and two pieces of Han pottery farm animals. On the table lie art books, novels and histories by authors of various nationalities. All have been read and everything has been studied. In the middle of the table there is a marvelous Han dynasty head of a horse. Against the walls there are marvelous pieces: a glass-fronted cabinet, another horse that dates from the Sui dynasty. There is also a Neolithic vase (2000-3000 B.C.), funerary figures, South East Asian vases and Thai ceramics. A side table displays a collection of Cambodian silver – a fish, a Nautilus shell and a sitting deer. Opposite the coffee table presides a fabulous bronze frog drum from Myanmar, used to summon rain. It is surrounded by a set of frogs that seem to lie in wait for the first raindrops.

In the second salon two chairs, known as chicken-wing-wood chairs, stand next to a wooden Tibetan prayer box. An early-20th century Senneh *kilim* dominates the library. Here, along the book shelves, are important works on Asia as well as books in English about contemporary history, social thought, globalization and religion. Early Singapore prints and an antique map hang on the wood panel walls of the library. The halls are lined with Cambodian silk tapestries. Two Han dynasty figures, their hands broken off, stand in a dining-room corner. Intact, they would be priceless. The dining table is different; very fine, very "Giacomettian", it is made of rosewood panels. The paintings by Singaporean artists on display are the property of the State and come from the collection of the Minis-

The library is also used as a music room. A Senneh "kilim" hangs on the wall. Draped over the sofa is a Sumba cloth from Indonesia.

Left
*Two Chinese calligraphy
rolls capture the attention.
The Myanmar frog drum,
used to summon rain and
surrounded by a set
of frogs, gives the
room an Asian tone.*

Opposite page
*The rosewood dining table
is set for lunch. The painting
in mixed media on the wall
is by Singaporean artist
Goh Beng Kwan.*

try of Foreign Affairs. The Ministry furnishes all the Singapore embassies around the world, in line with the cultural policy of the Government. They are distinguished from the ones that belong to Ambassador Heng-Chee Chan by their distinctive gold frames.

She has a doctorate in political science and with her first paycheck, bought what she had always dreamt of having: a painting by her fellow Singaporean, Arthur Yap, the poet, artist and writer. The painting holds the place of honor in the salon. After the first prized work, came the antique textiles and the Persian rugs. She is an expert on textile arts, and a large part of her collection, built up over the years, always travels with her, as we see in the residence.

We return to the vestibule of palms and shells at the bottom of the staircase. "What is key to this house, to all its furnishings and objects, is the fusion of the East and the West," concludes Ambassador Chan, who gave us a guided tour of the mansion.

Left
The eye travels from the grand Persian rug to the aluminum relief by the Singaporean artist, Sim Kern Teck, over the chimney, then it comes back and stops at the perfect Chinese Han dynasty head of a horse at the center of the table.

Above
The vestibule gives us the first clue as to which objects play a central role in the residence's décor: rugs, palms, sculptures, paintings and shells.

SOUTH AFRICA

Ralph Close, the then South African Minister (Chief of Legation), and prime mover behind the establishment of South Africa's own chancery and residence, imposed just one condition for this building: it had to be simple, yet dignified, so that his compatriots would feel reasonably proud of it. To give it this identity, the team in charge of the project included, not only the diplomat himself, but also John Whelan (who designed this house and its neighbor, the home of the Norwegian legation) and Charles Tompkins, the wealthy builder and owner of the original mansion that is today the splendid residence of the Peruvian ambassador. South Africa's site was purchased in 1935 in the Pretty Prospect district.

If you only glance at it while passing by, and have no architectural knowledge, you might think this mansion is just one more residence on Embassy Row. That would be the first mistake. The façade alone merits the attention of the informed passerby, because of its "Cape Dutch" style, even though here limestone replaces the whitewashed plaster walls that typify the old houses of Cape Town. Also of interest are the undulating gables of the dormers and the "Kat Balcony", a scale replica of the one constructed in Cape Town in the 17th century by the Dutch East India Company. The glazed and tinted glass of the main door and the four fluted pilasters of the façade are characteristic of the 18th century buildings of South Africa.

When the door opens, a new world unfolds before the visitor. The monotone uniformity of the stone outside changes completely, thanks to the vestibule's tribal dolls, which display multi-colored skirts, headdresses, bracelets, woven textiles and beads – an introduction to the variety of handicrafts made in the country's nine regions. The great hall that comes next is different: the dominant tones here are the black and white of the 27 engravings, each by a different South African artist, that depict the country's new Charter of Human Rights.

The difference between pre- and post-liberation South Africa shows itself in other aspects of the house. On the frontispiece of the façade, for example, the embassy has yet to replace the old coat of arms, a gift from the Close family, which will be a complicated process since it is carved into the stone. On the second floor, the difference between the furniture and the objects of the drawing room and those of the reception room is marked indeed. While in the former, the colonial atmosphere is retained (even the china kept in the armoire bears the engraving of the old shield), in the latter the country's new unification is stressed by the new shield and the diversity of the handicrafts, paintings, basketry, and textiles that decorate it. They speak of a country eager for any opportuny to express itself. For example, the indescribable *Ndebeles* dolls and the Christmas tree, a *baobab* upon whose phantasmagoric branches hang all types of wooden animals, huts, dolls, and masks. However, the most fascinating aspect of the tree is the explanation for its peculiar form of foliage: it appears that in an attack of frivolity, the gods decided to crown it with roots, and here is the result.

In the Ambassador's Lounge, the country's unification after liberation is emphasized and embodied by the new shield and the diversity of handicrafts, paintings, basketry, and textiles that decorate it. They speak of a country eager to express itself. The majority of the furniture is in the traditional South African style.

The wood used for the dining room tables and walls, the ambassador's writing desk, and the various *armoires* and bookcases found about the house is a story in itself. Called "stinkwood" because of the strong odor that penetrates the air as soon as it is cut, its commercial use has been banned for the past 200 years, in order to halt its impending extinction. Only the South African embassy in London contains a similar room. While this table can seat 24 people, the one in the blue room, which follows, is reserved for more intimate dinners.

And now for the staircase. Perhaps Mr. Whelan experienced a dream state and god-like moment when he designed it, because the truth is that it came out as stunningly as the *baobab*. From a paired grand staircase on the first floor, it rises to a single set of stairs on the second floor, reclaims its two arms on the third, and finishes with one on the fourth. In the end, there is no staircase or landing which does not remind us that we are in South African territory. That is a great achievement in Washington's sea of residences, where not every house achieves this unique effect.

SPAIN

Today, this mansion probably would have been the home of the Vice-President of the United States- if only First Lady Florence Harding and the U.S. Congress had approved the plan. Or it might have become the residence of Mexico's ambassadors, if the Mexican government had been tempted by the offer. Because of these mysterious complications of history, the house that the Embassy of Spain now occupies in Washington took a while to find its destiny, but when it did, it remained firmly in place and from that day onward – unlike many other residences – its ownership has not changed hands.

The mansion was one of many that Mary Foote Henderson commissioned the architect George Oakley Totten Jr. to design. Determined to renovate the sector, this stubborn wife of an ex-senator from Missouri managed to convince the city authorities to re-christen her street as the "Avenue of Presidents." But the initiative didn't last long: the neighbors protested because they had to change the address on their stationery and also because it became a nuisance to have to find the newly-named street when logic dictated it should lie, between 15th and 17th streets.

And there weren't only numerical conflicts to deal with. Totten designed the house, unlike others, without a specific country in mind, and the result, according to the experts, was a "strictly American" style. For others, the style seemed a mixture of Venetian palace and California Mission, but both sides agreed that this house was not one of Totten's greatest achievements. A tenacious and practical woman, Mrs. Henderson offered the house as a gift to the federal government for the home of the Vice-President of the United States. She made this offer in 1923, shortly after the house was completed. The house is too big for a Vice-President, President Harding's wife concluded; the Vice-President's salary isn't enough for the upkeep, Congress added. As a second try, it was offered as the ideal residence for the Mexican government, but that government finally opted to purchase the MacVeagh mansion instead.

The house remained empty for three years, awaiting a more dignified fate. Then, in 1926, the Spanish government sent over Ambassador Alejandro Padilla, with a clear instruction to purchase a permanent seat in Washington, and the formerly disdained property of 16th Street was his choice. Until that point, they had rented another "Henderson house" two blocks away. The ambassador and his wife took on the renovation and embellishment of the house, as well as the building of a chancery in the back of the residence. Totten was not the architect for this project, but rather Jules Henri de Sibour, who designed the French and Colombian embassies, among other buildings. The plans proposed ample offices on the ground floor, with the private quarters on the higher floors.

According to chronicles of the time, the original property passed through various stages of renovation. In agreement with the particular tastes and needs of succeeding diplomats, some basic comforts were added : a big kitchen, an elevator, and a good garage. A special place was occupied by an indoor patio – also called a conservatory – in the classic Andalusian

Patio Conservatory. Both the dining room and the sitting room open onto this interior patio. It was remodeled in 1927; fine hand-painted tiles were brought over from Valencia and Sevilla. The wrought iron grilles came from Toledo. In 1955 the glass-vaulted roof was covered for practical reasons. Eastern and southeastern exposures constantly flood the space with natural light. The cast iron columns support the lantern arches and create a large indoor gazebo, with a fountain in the center. The tile painting of "Nuestra Señora de los Reyes", placed on the back wall, adds a typically Spanish touch to the room.

Opposite page and right
Between impressive columns, a beautiful 17th century Flemish tapestry covers the west wall of the ballroom or "Red Room." It was further remodeled three times: in 1952, 1955 and again in 1965. During the years of the Spanish Civil War it was used as a storage room.

style, with a fountain in the middle, hand-painted tiles from Sevilla and Valencia, and grilles made in Toledo.

With the ending of the monarchy in 1931 and the Spanish Civil War, the residence would suffer reflectively from the political turbulence of the times and fall into a sad abandonment. One anecdote tells how a mosaic of Nuestra Señora de los Reyes (the patron saint of Sevilla), on one of the patio walls, was covered in cement during the term of Fernando de los Rios, the ambassador in Washington from 1936 through 1939. And the ballroom was used for years as a storage room.

In the decade of the 1950's, the mansion received a better and well-deserved care, while José María Areilza was the Ambassador. The ballroom was redecorated in a French style, with walls of abundant white and gold, large mirrors and heavy chandeliers. In this same room, which is the most important in the residence, Areilza re-hung the imposing portraits of King Alfonso XIII and Queen Victoria Eugenia, which had been taken down at

The red damask-covered walls add warmth to such a large room. The four crystal chandeliers were added in 1955. Paintings from the Prado Museum hang in the ballroom. Two are portraits of Queen Isabel de Farnesio, the wife of Philip V, including the oval one over the mantel.

the end of the monarchy. Today many other paintings by celebrated Spanish artists, on loan from the Prado Museum, along with seventeenth century Flemish tapestries, adorn the walls of more than one room of the house. After a long and profound search for a destiny and an identity, Spain is the home's owner, and it shows.

After all, the "casona" or great house on 16th Street, as it is affectionately called by Spaniards, is about to finish its first vital cycle, seventy-five years after the Government of Spain acquired it for the residence of its ambassadors to Washington. A more modern diplomatic seat, better-located on the map of the capital, will be its replacement. Mrs. Henderson's building will go on to serve other functions. It is not the first time that one of the small palaces on 16th Street has gone through a transition of this kind. Before Spain, Mexico, Italy and Poland had to seek other homes for their representatives.

The current ambassador Javier Rupérez and his wife Rakela are contemplating the move with a certain nostalgia, but they leave happily, in the knowledge that the Spanish government has destined the great house on 16th street for the Cervantes Institute. This is a fine choice for the walls that for so long, and in such a variety of circumstances, served to house the dignity of Spain.

Left

This room is in the 19th century English Regency style, which incorporated delicate classical moldings and statuary niches. Folding glazed doors open onto the patio conservatory. To strengthen the impact of the conservatory, the wall opposite the doors is mirrored in a design of square panes. An impressive twelve-light crystal chandelier draws the eye to the center of the room. When fully extended, the dining room table can comfortably seat thirty.

Above

There is a marvelous rug woven by the Royal Tapestry Works in Madrid (La Real Fábrica de Tapices de Madrid) and the chandelier is from the famous La Granja crystal works near Segovia. The 18th century Flemish tapestry was originally woven for the Royal Palace in Madrid.

SWEDEN

Built in 1923 by the respected architect Arthur B. Heaton for David Lawrence, the founder of *U.S. News and World Report*, this mansion was acquired by the Swedish government in 1950. The obvious question one asks oneself while standing before the façade is: "What does this Spanish-style house have in common with Sweden so that it was chosen to be the residence of its ambassadors?" The answer is: little, and yet much. Apart from the abundance and the beauty of the green space that surrounds it, the house possesses two characteristics that are key in the aesthetic of its resident country: simplicity and light. These same characteristics are found, in various proportions, throughout the house. Although the decoration one finds in the principal salon is in the *Gustavian* style (named for King Gustav III, 1746-1792), which at first sight has nothing to do with the contemporary style of the sunroom, the former is as simple, linear and luminous as the latter. This is not unusual, because, throughout the intense, successful and varied history of Swedish design, tradition and modernity have always gone hand in hand. Just as was firmly established in 1992, when the Nobel Foundation especially commissioned a complete banquet dinner service for the 90th anniversary of the prizes. After interminable debates, the result was beautiful, and not too surprising: a masterful blend of the old and the new.

Here again, the objects speak of crucial moments in the history of taste in the country. In the library, for example, the daring fabric choice for the sofa and its matching chairs makes the strongest statement. It was designed by Josef Frank, an Austrian architect who arrived in Stockholm in 1930 and made history with his very personal vision in furniture, lamps, glasswork and textiles.

Calm returns in the classic dining room. The very Swedish Orrefors crystal sits on an English mahogany rococo table under the cut-crystal baroque chandelier, framing the no less traditional Rörstrands china made exclusively for the residences of Swedish ambassadors.

Nevertheless, the space that leads the visitor to the best reflection of the country's aesthetic is the sunroom, completely furnished with pieces designed by Swedish artists. The room invites the visitor to follow the path that these artists traveled along to arrive at their designs. It reminds us of the declaration of principles made by the aesthete Ellen Kay, who called for "Beauty in everything" in 1899, and another by Gregor Paulsson, a key figure of Swedish design, who demanded "Design for everyone, not just for the rich" in 1919. From there it was only a step to the elegance and grace that typified Swedish objects, and to the apotheosis of Functionalism, which promoted mass production, simple and practical forms and colors, and the rational use of space.

Since that time, Swedish design has evolved in accordance with the public's needs. Sweden's succcess at international exhibitions, joint efforts with other Scandinavian countries and the demands of globalization have transformed its design. It entered the new century with unfurled sails: "Made in Sweden" has become a byword for originality, quality and beauty. Fortunately, neither the residence, nor the pot handle, nor the sweater's stitch, to say nothing of the Aquavit, is free of Sweden's all-encompassing aesthetic.

In the library the daring fabric choice for the sofa and its matching chairs makes the strongest statement. It was designed by Josef Frank, an Austrian architect who arrived in Stockholm in 1930 and made history with his very personal vision in furniture, lamps, glasswork and textiles. Over the chimney hangs "Attacking Goshawk," a painting by Bruno Liljefors (1860-1939), a renowned Swedish artist who specialized in depictions of wildlife.

Opposite page
*The Gustavian style of the
principal salon includes the
furnishings, the mirror and
the ceiling light. The tapestry
is a portrait of King Gustav III
by an unknown artist.*

Above
*The decoration one
finds in the principal salon
is in the Gustavian style
(named for King
Gustav III, 1746-1792).
Although, at first sight,*

*it has nothing to do with
the contemporary style
of the sunroom, the former
is as simple, linear, and
luminous as the latter.*

Above

*This space, known as the
sunroom, is completely
furnished with pieces by
contemporary Swedish
designers. The ceramic
lamps are by the artist
Cilla Adlercreutz.
The painting in the
background is the work
of Björn Wessman.*

Right

*The very Swedish Orrefors
crystal sits on an English
mahogany rococo table,
under the cut-crystal baroque
chandelier, framing the no
less traditional Rörstrands
china made exclusively for
the residences of Swedish
ambassadors. In the
background, the painting is
by the Swedist artist Elias
Martin (1739-1818).*

THE NETHERLANDS

It is not a matter of tulips. If the tulip were the way to the Dutch Embassy residence, there would be massive confusion. The famous Dutch symbol is found in abundance all over Washington during the month of March. What makes a difference, what is definitively fabulous, is the great variety of species that one finds in The Netherlands diplomatic seat. At the beginning of spring, all must take the obligatory stroll by the S Street front garden to see and admire the tulips. And not just to esteem them, but also to learn their names: the Farah tulip is named for Farah Diba, the former Empress of Iran; the Elizabeth is for the Queen of England. One must not forget that every time a head of state visits Holland, a new species is baptized with his or her name.

As for the house itself and its furnishings, it is not quite clear whether anything remains of Louis Septimus Ownsley's era. Ownsley was the Chicago native who was its original proprietor. It is clear, nevertheless, that it was this "Baron of Traction" – Ownsley's nickname, because his fortune was in trolley cars – who asked the architect Ward Brown to design a Neo-Classical Revival mansion for him 1929. Wilmar Bolling, the brother of Woodrow Wilson's second wife, was in charge of the construction. The former President of the United States lived just across the street after his presidency. Ownsley, in contrast, decided to retire to Connecticut and sell his valuable, 30-room piece of real estate to the Dutch government.

At the beginning of the 1990s, it became evident that the mansion was in dire need of renovation, for aesthetic and practical reasons. The magnificent collection of paintings was emphasized and enhanced, in order to give a broader perspective on the art of the Netherlands.

From the beginning, the mansion's renovation and restoration was an international enterprise. It took a full five years to complete! And only in 1999 were the Ambassador, his family and the mansion's personnel able to move back into the residence. The engineering and architectural works required a complex collaboration between Dutch firms and their U.S. counterparts. Even though they were separated by an ocean, they were insistent on achieving one common objective: to return the mansion to its original splendor.

Among all of the work that was undertaken, complex systems of temperature and humidity control and special lighting were installed in the salons where the valuable paintings, sculptures, original furnishings, silk and wool tapestries, Delftware (the unmistakable blue-and-white Dutch ceramics) and antiques were exhibited. The mansion was gradually transformed into a small, but stunning, private museum. At the same time, and always respecting the original design, its spaces were upgraded so that the hosts could offer an intimate dinner or a reception for 300 in a comfortable setting.

Everywhere, one can see the rewards of the effort that was undertaken. It is impossible to ignore the three imposing green and white marble arches on the

Great marble staircase patterned after that of the Petit Trianon in the Palace of Versailles.

Opposite page and above

As no other genre can, portraits provide a colorful description of the different periods of history and the Dutch are its recognized masters. Over the chimney in the library hangs a portrait of the Prince of Orange, from the studio of Gerard van Honthorst (1590-1656), a leading portraitist of the School of Utrecht.

second level's exterior. The great marble staircase is in the limestone entrance hall; its banister is a copy of the one at Marie Antoinette's Petit Trianon in the Palace of Versailles. There are decorative urns in every corner and open space and pediments at the threshold of the principal salon and the dining room. There are "Adamesque" touches everywhere. These details are the trademark of the talented brothers Robert and James Adam, the Scottish architects who designed many public and private buildings in Scotland and England towards the end of the 18th century.

The fine wood and plasterwork of the dining room and principal salons have been stripped of their heavy coats of paint and lightened with fresh colors and textures. A pair of oak and glass doors that face a wide terrace were added to the high, polychrome-ceilinged library. The third floor has new private quarters for the ambassador's family and for Her Majesty, The Queen, when she visits Washington.

Left

The ambassador's residence has to serve both as a home and as a showcase for the rich artistic and cultural traditions of the country. When the restoration was undertaken, the Dutch government made sure that the lighting and the systems of humidity and temperature control complied with the strictest standards, to provide optimum conditions for the preservation of the valuable collection of paintings, sculptures and tapestries.

Above

A sitting area in the drawing room. The painting is Landscape near Leiden, *by Anthony van der Croos (1603-1663).*

As they walk through each room of the residence, visitors are shown the various genres of the art of the Netherlands, such as landscapes, still lifes and portraits. But it is in the dining room where they find examples of each and every one of the main themes of Dutch art, in the works of Dusart, van Dijk, Storck, van Beerstraten and Adriana Johanna Haanen, among others.

THE PEOPLE'S REPUBLIC OF CHINA

It has been said that East is East and West is West. But a visit to the residence of the Ambassador of The People's Republic of China confirms that there is a rich meeting ground between the two. To begin with, though there is no apparent external sign – call it a flag or a seal – that tells you that you are in front of the diplomatic seat of this nation. People who understand Chinese culture know full well the importance of the door. In fact, the great teak door that welcomes the visitor was designed and made to measure for this western-style house, along with its message. The traditional symmetric carving signifies happiness, good luck, protection and harmony.

And it is always with this thought in mind that one must travel through the residence. One must always go beyond the objects themselves. One must understand that lotuses signify summer; the chrysanthemum, fall; the peony, spring; the plum tree, winter; and vermilion, happiness and good omens. It is not enough to know that the mansion was built in 1931 by the architectural firm of Frost and Ganger for the Stern-Burroughs marriage and that China acquired it on the 30th of July 1973. The initial repairs, *de rigueur* and minor, were done immediately after the purchase. The real work came later. The huge renovations, which took over a year, were only finished in September of 2001 and they included the whitewashing of the façade – manually and with workmen brought over from China – to return the bricks to their original red.

The ambassador returned on the 9th day of the 9th month to inhabit the home on S Street. The date was not chosen at random, but in the knowledge that the number nine is a lucky one.

And we are back in the land of symbols. The principal drawing room has two clearly demarcated spaces, in accordance with the nation's policy of opening itself to the outside world. One is the traditional Chinese-style room, with mahogany and marble furnishings. At the other end, there is an elegant European-style salon, where the cushioning of the pieces contrasts with the "verticality" of the Asian ones. The same thing occurs in the dining room: the table is set with silverware and crystal in the western manner, and next to them are the delicately-placed chopsticks of the East.

The same general scheme is repeated in the recent addition, an immense and luminous reception hall. It was designed by a local architect and built by a Chinese company. The hall has a view of the pool and the tennis court.

There are few concessions to the West in the artwork, *objets d'art* and cuisine. China makes its presence felt in the jades, calligraphy, tea, porcelain, lacquerwork, and marble of the floors and chairs. The latter were one of the huge surprises of the visit. If the ambassador's wife had not pointed it out, we would have gone home convinced that the delicate landscapes that decorate the marble chair backs were painted by human hands and not by Mother Nature. The dark veins of the stone rise towards what seem to be the Himalayas, and then descend abruptly until they come up against the valleys, where they mingle with the pine tops, as though they had been painted in brushstrokes.

The golden arches in relief that cross the ceiling are a dazzling feature of the principal foyer. Note the strong contrast between the dark green walls and the generous amounts of marble seen in the floor, the doorframes and the niches. Everything is made in China.

Page 286
Facing the entrance of the dining room there is a painting of flowers and birds by the renowned artist Ren Bonian. The table is set with silverware and crystal in the Western manner, but the delicately-placed chopsticks of the East are also present.

The secrets of jade were revealed as we observed the profusion of pieces on the dining room shelves. They are classified, according to their color, as emerald, white, green, agate, crystal and coral jade. It is not just a matter of polishing the stone. Its natural form must be respected and accentuated, as well as its grain, texture and color. We also learned that Beijing jade – celebrated for the brilliance of its colors – is not the same as the innovative stonework from Guangzhou – where the artist's creativity and imagination are totally respected – nor the more sophisticated pieces from Shanghai.

Calligraphy was the topic in the drawing and reception rooms, where we warmed ourselves with a few cups of tea, the national drink and one of the most important unifying links among the fifty-six ethnic groups that inhabit the country. We discovered – after the idea was translated for Western ears and greatly simplified – that the plainer and more lineal the sign, the more complicated it is to maintain its internal equilibrium. The contrary is also true, the more strokes involved in the symbol, the easier it is to trace. So, while East does meet West, diversity makes up this colorful world.

The principal drawing room in the residence of the Ambassador of the People's Republic of China has two clearly demarcated spaces, in accordance with his country's policy of opening itself to the outside world. One is the traditional Chinese-style room with mahogany and marble furnishings. At the other end, there is an elegant European-style salon. The Chinese space is presided over by a work of the famous calligrapher Liu Bingsheng.

THE REPUBLIC OF KOREA

The Republic of Korea selected the beautiful Spring Valley neighborhood to build its ambassador's residence. In 1977, the lot was purchased for $570 000. The construction of the residence began in 1984 and was completed two years later at a cost exceeding $5.6 million. That same year, an adjacent lot was acquired from its neighbor, American University, to enlarge the gardens. The transaction was finalized in 1996.

Kim Su-guen, the legendary Korean architect of the Space Institute and the principal planner of the Seoul Olympic Complex for the 1988 games, designed the residence. The Washington architect, Jack Samperton, oversaw the construction. Sadly, Mr. Kim passed away a few months before the opening reception took place.

The atmosphere created by the marble, parquet floors, crystal chandeliers, Louis XVI furnishings, ironwork and Aubusson rugs of other ambassadors' residences in Washington contrasts sharply with the wood, rice paper, bamboo, pagodas, lanterns and stones of the Korean ambassador's residence.

The combination of light, space, serenity and intimacy were elements interwoven to create the subdued elegance of the residence. The use of these elements followed the architectural models of the *Baek-je* Kingdom (18 B.C.-600 A.D.) that influenced later Japanese architecture.

The geometric shapes of the latticed doors and the lamps are also reminiscent of the styles of this period. Kim departed from the traditional tile roof with the use of copper. He felt that the green patina the metal acquired with age would harmonize better with the natural surrounding.

Order and neatness prevail indoors. The saying that Korean architecture is more sober than that of China, but less austere than its Japanese counterpart, seems apropriate here. The colors are subdued, but the many paintings decorating the walls burst with bright colors.

The spacious inner courtyard displays a singular beauty. Large, tall, brown clay pots traditionally used to store soybean paste (*doenjang*), red pepper bean paste (*gochujang*), and *kimchee*, the fermented vegetable dish which is a basic staple of Korean food, now serve as decoration in a corner of the courtyard. The latticed doors and windows of rice paper (*chanjoi*), constructed and installed by Korean artisans, lend the courtyard a uniquely Korean atmosphere.

Across the central courtyard is a large garden with a waterfall. From the wooden pavilion, a stream meanders through the garden and culminates in a waterfall. Water lilies, lotuses and other aquatic flowers dot the stream, cascading into a pond at the bottom of the waterfall. Carp swim around the stream, below the wooden bridge above the waterfall.

For centuries, people in Korea have recognized the importance of nature in their lives. Thus, water, trees and hills must surround any good Korean home. These elements were skillfully employed to evoke a sense of serenity and harmony in this graceful residence.

Three large lamps made of rice paper and delicate wooden frames hang in the foyer. Traditional lamps with cloud motifs line the walls leading to the grand Reception Hall. The Chinese characters in the center of the rug symbolize happiness. Brightly-colored oil paintings by Namgye grace the walls of the foyer.

Left and above
*The inner courtyard possesses
a serene beauty. In one corner
are rows of decorative
earthenware jars for storing
sauces and pickled vegetables.
The double-tiered roof and
the beams are classic examples
of period architecture. Stone
sculptures, including the
Haetae, an imaginary marine
animal and harbinger of good
fortune, crouch in the
courtyard. They are also
scattered throughout the
gardens, to guard against
the intrusion of evil spirits.*

Opposite page
A large stone stands in the middle of the courtyard. Stones are frequently used in Korean homes as a reminder of nature. The geometric tiles surrounding the stones accentuate the Baek-je period decoration.

Right
The shadows cast by the roof highlight the changhoji windows, contributing to the contemplative atmosphere treasured in the countries of the Far East.

Left

In this grand room, special events and celebrations are hosted for distinguished guests. The décor of the room integrates traditional and modern elements. The windows and lamps were fashioned after the models and motifs found in ancient Korean palaces and temples. Creating an atmosphere of dignity and serenity, the overall design of this room accentuates openness and spaciousness, with its high ceiling and traditional-style beams.

Above

The windows are made of wood and changhoji, *rice paper. Bamboo blinds,* bal, *serve both decorative and functional purposes. Lattice-patterned wooden panels, characteristic of traditional Korean architecture, are found above the windows and decorate the upper portion of walls throughout the residence.*

TUNISIA

The sight of a white house perched on top of a hill, as you drive through Rock Creek Park, immediately transports you to the Mediterranean. Even though it was not specifically built for its embassy, Tunisia's is neither the first nor the only ambassadorial residence in this city that has so much in common with the nation whose home it would become. The residence´s style is a perfect match for the architecture of this country on the shores of the Mediterranean.

The Embassy of Tunisia ´s first owner had lived with his family in Portugal and, when one of his daughters married (around the 1920s), he had a home built in the Mediterranean style that the girl liked so much. It turned out that the girl was nostalgic for the original and she promptly returned to Portugal. Tunisia acquired it in 1956, when it established diplomatic relations with the United States, and since then it has been the official home of its ambassadors.

The arcs and the *torsade* carved columns contribute to its Mediterranean look, as does the intricately-carved detail on the top of the exterior white walls, which contrasts with the vivid blue of the metalwork, echoing the classic houses of Sidi Bou Said, a picturesque Tunisian fishing village declared by UNESCO to be a "World Heritage" site. The Tunisian national identity is present in each and every one of the interior rooms: in the paintings, the Ottoman-influenced lamps, the low leather furniture and the beautiful *Marfaa* – the antique carved and painted wooden *étagère* with encrusted glass that was used to hang swords and rifles.

Nevertheless, and as is to be expected, the rugs are the dominant element. Their worldwide renown is amply justified. Some of the more stunning carpets are from Kairouan, a holy town located 160 kms from the capital, Tunis. This town was the capital of the country during the *Aghlabite* dynasty (800-900 A.D.) as well as a major cultural, intellectual and spiritual center of the Mediterranean region.

The famous Kairouan rugs, like the impressive example in gold and blue tones in the Grand Salon of the residence, are hand-knotted from pure lamb's wool. The carpet in the Tunisian salon is an *Alloucha*, essentially a typical Kairouan design, with a central geometrical medallion and hand-knotted, but with the color limitation imposed by using only the natural tones of the lamb's wool.

When you visit the *Souks*, the colorful Tunisian markets, you will learn to differentiate the different types of carpets and their respective qualities, from classical rugs to *Kilims*, *Mergoums* and the rugs made of silk. Connoisseurs catalog as "normal" a rug whose weave has between 10 and 40 thousand knots per square meter. A "fine" one has between 65 and 90 thousand knots, and an "extra fine" rug somewhere between 160 and 500 thousand knots. Silk rugs can have over 500 thousand knots per square meter.

Tunisia, a crossroads of several civilizations and a country known for its long and rich history of over 4000 years, has an exquisite handicraft tradition. The ceramics, for example, have been famous since antiquity, some dating as far back as Punic and Roman times. Craftsmen constantly perfected this art, adding colors and forms enriched by influences from Andalusia, Italy and the Arab Levant. Today it is a vibrant industry and an important part of Tunisia's palette of craft and decorative arts.

The long shape of the Salon Tunisien *recalls the outlines of a room in a traditional Tunisian patio house, explains Faika S. Atallah, a great hostess and the wife of the ambassador. On the wall is an ancient carved and painted wooden* étagère, *encrusted with mirrors. It is called a* Marfaa *and was used to hang rifles and swords. A beautiful traditional carpet, of the* Alloucha *variety, covers the floor. The antique bronze floor-lamp is of Oriental inspiration and depicts a man with a head turban holding a* torchere.

Above

A spiral staircase with forged ironwork details. The arches with torsade columns and a traditional brass and glass ceiling lamp are of clear Ottoman influence. On the back wall, a carved and pierced plaster architectural detail.

Right

Above the sofa, a painting by Tunisian master Jalel Ben Abdallah (1921-). The painter was one of the founding members of "L'École de Tunis" artistic movement. The centerpiece of the room is a magnificent gold and blue hand-knotted carpet in the classic Kairouan design. The name comes from a holy town, 160 kms from the capital, Tunis. This town was the capital of the country during the Aghlabite dynasty (800-900 A.D.) and one of the cultural, spiritual and intellectual centers of the Mediterranean. Today, it is still home to the famous Kairouan carpets.

TURKEY

The elegant gray stone mansion at Sheridan Circle and 23rd street, N.W., has long been the residence of the ambassador of Turkey. The architectural design is a fusion of design elements spanning three centuries. The striking façade, with its fluted columns, paneled balustrades, and an elaborate portico, appears to have been made to order for its long-term residents – the nation recognized as the bridge between Europe and Asia. The neoclassical interior, heightened by decorative ceilings, elaborate carvings and stained-glass windows, is also well suited to the country, a place where the cultures of East and West have met for centuries.

George Oakley Totten, Jr., a Washington architect, was hired by the industrialist Edward Hamlin Everett to build a mansion for him, and was given a free hand to spend and to dream. Work on the building began in 1914. It was made out of brick, and granite from Bowling Green, Ohio, Everett's native state.

Totten's work was inspired by the time he spent in Istanbul. His work on the first American chancery in Turkey and the residence of the Prime Minister, Izzet Pasha, won recognition from Sultan Abdul-Hamid, who offered Totten the position of "personal and private architect to the Sultan" in 1908. But Abdul-Hamid lost his throne in 1909 before their partnership even began. After Totten finished the mansion in 1915, Everett moved in and furnished his new residence with Louis XVI and Regency pieces, oriental and Aubusson rugs, fine paintings, and rare pieces of art.

In the decade immediately following World War I, Everett and his wife, Grace Burnap, were hosts of the "Evenings with Music" galas. Hundreds of Washington socialites gathered each week to hear the music of opera stars and concert pianists. The tradition continued until Everett's death in 1929.

Three years later, the Turkish government leased the house from Everett's widow and became the proud owner of the fully-furnished mansion in 1936. Personal possessions of successive envoys and their wives, such as crystal and rugs, have intermittently enhanced the permanent collection of Turkish art that adorns the interior.

In the 1940's, Ahmet Ertegun, son of the Turkish Ambassador M.N. Ertegun, invited his friends and jazz aficionados to the residence for luncheons which featured jam sessions by musicians from bands like Duke Ellington's and Louis Armstrong's. Those events, which gave great delight, eventually led to the founding of Atlantic Records.

The entrance is a bronze-grille double door, giving way to the hall of the mansion. This welcoming area is rich in Doric columns and architraves. The gray-veined white marble floor is accented by sienna and mint geometric patterns. *Capo di Monde* urns rest atop the domineering white marble mantelpiece.

To the left of the hall is the office of the residence and to the right is the Ambassador's study. The latter is filled with lavish furnishings, such as a Persian rug, an elegant desk, and luxurious sofas and chairs, recently reupholstered in a classic gold and cream pattern.

The staircase, with its elaborately-carved banister, ascends to the mid-landing. Here, in front of the stained-glass window off the alcove, once stood the bust of Mustafa Kemal

The large marble fireplace on the north wall is flanked by two sets of double doors that open to the drawing room. The north triangle of the drawing room is set off from the rest of the room by chiseled columns. The stark white walls and ceiling highlight the large beige, rose and blue Aubusson carpet.

A wrought-iron trellis gate in the ballroom leads to a tranquil solarium. Its fully-windowed alcove, featuring stained glass panels, allows for abundant natural lighting. An antique Turkish rug spans the length of the room, and the walls bear a corresponding tile-motif.

Ataturk, national hero and founder of the republic. The sculpture has since been moved up the street to the chancery on Massachusetts Avenue.

A large reception room is reached by a divided staircase, which is lined by two 16th century wall-paintings by Bronzino. The teakwood floor was imported from China and is adorned with a Turkish carpet. The ceiling is edged with a carved Corinthian design and two antique brass chandeliers hang from it. A massive mahogany table rests on the carpet in the center of the room. Between the landings of the staircases is a Turkish bronze brazier, topped by symbolic crescents.

The staircase, with its elaborately carved banister, ascends to the mid-landing. Here, in front of the stained glass window off the alcove, once stood the bust of Mustafa Kemal Ataturk, national hero and founder of the republic. The sculpture has since been moved up the street to the chancery on Massachusetts Avenue.

The large marble fireplace on the north wall is flanked by two sets of double doors that open onto the drawing room. The north triangle of the drawing room is set off from the rest of the room by chiseled columns. The stark white walls and ceiling highlight the large beige, rose and blue Aubusson carpet. The regal gold draperies emphasize the handsomely-upholstered Louis XVI and Regency furniture. Two exquisite crystal chandeliers dangle graciously from the ceiling.

To the south of the reception room is a spectacular ballroom. The double doors are host to an ornate, circular lattice embellishment. Straight ahead, the stage, framed by Corinthian

Left

In the ballroom, the upper portion of the walls is covered by panels of gold and crimson Persian damask. Nine ceiling panels are divided by magnificently carved beams, and accentuated by gold and teal enamel. Red velvet draperies and upholstered chairs complete the room's grandiose atmosphere.

Above

To the south of the reception room is a spectacular ballroom. The double doors are host to an ornate, circular lattice embellishment.

columns, proudly displays a grand piano. The east wall is dominated by a massive built-in mirror, which is also outlined with columns. The upper portion of the walls is covered by panels of gold and crimson Persian damask. Nine ceiling panels are divided by magnificently carved beams, and accentuated by gold and teal enamel. Red velvet draperies and upholstered chairs complete the room's grandiose atmosphere.

A wrought-iron trellis gate in the ballroom leads to a tranquil solarium. Its fully-windowed alcove, featuring stained-glass panels, allows for abundant natural lighting. An antique Turkish rug spans the length of the room, and the walls bear a corresponding tile-motif.

Through the solarium archway is the dining room. Mirroring that arch on the north wall is a raised wooden dado, *which serves as a base for the recessed buffet shelf. A baroque pink and white floral fabric covers the walls. Three sets of double doors allow access to the reception room, the northwest pantry and the corridor.*

Through the solarium archway is the dining room. Mirroring that arch on the north wall is a raised wooden *dado*, which serves as a base for the recessed buffet shelf. A baroque pink and white floral fabric covers the walls. Three sets of double doors allow access to the reception room, the northwest pantry, and the corridor.

Immediately across the corridor from the dining room is the sitting room. The most impressive feature of this room is the china cupboard. Built in to the north wall, its three bays of prism-pane glass provide a handsome display case. There is yet another white marble fireplace here, supporting a remarkable gold Parisian clock. Regency sofas and chairs, covered with slate and rose toned upholstery, are the dominant furnishings. The third floor of the residence is designated as the private quarters for the Ambassador and his family. The quarters consist of a sitting room, four large bedrooms and four bathrooms.

The tiled roof-garden over the ballroom provides a fantastic view of the city. The basement houses a swimming pool.

Throughout the residence, doorknobs, locks and hinges are gold-plated, highlighting Everett's desire for opulence. The house is a grand and fitting home for the Turkish nation.

Immediately across the corridor from the dining room is the sitting room. There is yet another white marble fireplace here, supporting a remarkable gold Parisian clock. Regency sofas and chairs, covered with slate – and rose – toned upholstery, are the dominant furnishings.

UNITED KINGDOM

In 1893 the British Legation became an Embassy. It was situated on Connecticut Avenue, before moving to the present site at 3100 Massachusetts Avenue. The architect, Sir Edwin Lutyens (1869-1944), had started drawing up plans for the new Washington Embassy while he was at work on the Viceroy's palace in New Delhi (1913-1939). Lutyens planned and constructed over 300 houses and buildings during his career. They were built in Britain, Belgium, Germany, France, Italy, Hungary, South Africa, and, of course, India.

The residence, which is built of red brick with stone dressings and has high roofs crowned by tall chimneys, suggests an English country house of the Queen Anne period. There are similarities to the Viceroy's Palace: among them, high ceilings, columns, mirrors, detailed door handles and window catches.

In due course the number of embassy staff grew too great for the offices in the Lutyens house. In 1957, Her Majesty The Queen opened the new Chancery in the same compound as the residence. The old Chancery was converted into staff apartments, some of which are used as offices for visiting ministers.

In 1973, the residence had air-conditioning and a new kitchen put in. Under the guidance of Lady Henderson in the early 1980s, the reception rooms and bedrooms were redecorated by several British designers. In 1999, under Lady Meyer's supervision, the drawing room, dining room and library were redecorated, using British and American fabrics. This was followed by the rewiring, plumbing, modernization and redecoration of the bedroom floor, as well as the cloakrooms on the ground floor.

The residence is joined to the original offices by a bridge forming a *porte-cochère* to the main entrance, which is concealed behind the former offices. Over the bridge is the Ambassador's library. On entering the residence there is a twin staircase made of Indiana limestone, the underside of which forms a magnificent double flying arch.

The floor of the main gallery is made of Vermont marble and Pennsylvania slate. It leads from the library, runs the length of the house, passing the ballroom, and continues between the drawing and dining room, ending at the West Door. The staircase which leads from the main gallery to the bedroom floor is circular with an *art déco* banister.

The main reception rooms include the dining room, which has a mahogany table and, when it is at full capacity, seats thirty-four; the ballroom, which is used for receptions, large dinners, conferences and concerts; and the elegant and luminous drawing room. The portico, with its massive limestone pillars, is intended as a specific reference to the traditional Virginia plantation house. It is an extension of the ballroom and sweeps onto the terrace and into the rose gardens. Over the years additions to the gardens have been made, namely, the Japanese garden, the secret garden, the cutting and herb garden.

There are two bronze sculptures by British artists in the gardens: "Single Form" by Dame Barbara Hepworth and "Sleeping Horse" by Dame Elisabeth Frink. Standing outside the garden on Massachusetts Avenue is a bronze statue of Sir Winston Churchill by William McVey of Ohio, which is on permanent loan from the English-Speaking Union.

At the entrance to the residence there is a twin staircase made of Indiana limestone, the underside of which forms a magnificent double flying arch.

Opposite page
Painting: Lady Gertrude Fitzpatrick, from the school of Sir Joshua Reynolds (1774-1841). Panel of 18th century Chinese wallpaper. The mirror (one of pair) is in the style of Chippendale. An ornamental George I carved giltwood console table (one of a pair). The Lavar Kirman carpet has panels of Islamic script with quotations from various Persian poets and prophets.

Right
The drawing room seen from the main gallery, showing two of the pillars with Corinthian capitals. Painting: The Red Tea Pot, *by Alexander Achanov (property of Lady Meyer).*

Above

The steel columns are painted to resemble scagliola, a composition marble invented in Roman times and extensively used in 18th century houses. The smoked glass panels are original to the house. The antique Austrian chandeliers came from the old residence, as did the great Tabriz palace carpet. The grandfather clock is carved mahogany, made by Joseph Redrick (London, 19th century). The carved plaster frieze, in the style of Grinling Gibbons (1648-1720), has motifs that are repeated in the ballroom and gallery.

Opposite page

The Gallery looking to the West Door. The black and white corridor is 167' long and paved with squares of Vermont marble and Pennsylvania slate.

Opposite page

The Library. The portrait of Sir Winston Churchill is by Julian Lamar. The Library is a nearly perfect cube, with wood panelling in Palladian symmetry. Fluted Corinthian pilasters emphasize its height, as does the deeply vaulted ceiling. The woodwork is of liquidambar, a variety of gum tree which thrives in California. The carvings at the pilaster level symbolize power, wealth and knowledge. There are six doors to the room. The cast design on the fireback was inspired by the effigy of St. George on the old five-shilling piece.

Right

The walnut chairs, side tables and mahogany dining table seats (which can accomodate 34 diners) are in various 18th century styles. Painting: Evening Landscape, *by George Smith (Chichester, 1714-1776). The silver, cutlery and candelabra were formerly at the British Embassies in Lisbon and The Hague and came to Washington in 1893, when the legation acquired Embassy status.*

VENEZUELA

Diógenes Escalante was Venezuela's first ambassador in Washington, and remained at the post for ten years. (Previously, Venezuela had designated plenipotentiary ministers). As a diplomat, he faced many challenges, but today he is recognized as a key figure in the task of supervising the construction and embellishment of the residence. He took this job very seriously. For months he maintained a copious correspondence with the Casa Amarilla – the Ministry of Foreign Relations in Venezuela – and informed them of every detail, giving a meticulous accounting of every expense, no matter how small. And in the middle of a cold Washington winter in February 1940, his stubbornness and patience were finally rewarded, when he hosted the lavish and elegant reception he had long been dreaming of. The inauguration of the mission was a recurring topic of conversation in the capital's most exclusive social circles that season.

He had wanted to open the doors of the residence months before, but there had been many obstacles to overcome: the ongoing construction worker's strike in Washington caused delays and the war in Europe held up the delivery of furniture specially ordered from France and Italy.

While the guest list was being drawn up in Washington, a steamship, the Santa Paula, sailed from the port of La Guaira on the central coast of Venezuela, carrying some anxiously-awaited cargo for Escalante. He was greatly relieved when he finally unwrapped these works of art, which included some of the greatest examples of 19th century Venezuelan painting. One by one they emerged: the celebrated "Miranda at the Carraca", by Arturo Michelena; the equally famous "Signing of the Act of Independence", by Tovar y Tovar; and a portrait of physician Jose María Vargas, an illustrious Venezuelan humanitarian. They were all copies, of course, painted by a talented compatriot, Alejandro d'Empayre. Empayre was a painter of such talent that he had once sold copies of Michelena as originals, which led to a huge criminal scandal.

Simultaneously, and in a race against time, another steamship, the Santa Rosa, anchored in New York harbor with yet another container destined for the Embassy of Venezuela's residence in Washington. The container held a marble bust of the Liberator, Simón Bolívar, a reproduction of the original by the eminent Italian sculptor Pietro Tenerani, which had stood before in the Tricolor Salon of the Foreign Ministry in Caracas. There was already a place especially reserved for the bust in the residence on Massachusetts Avenue.

The construction of the embassy residence – the first Latin American one to be built in the capital – cost $200 000 and the New York architect Chester A. Patterson designed it. The decision to build it was made after a long round of visits to the houses available on the market – the chancery, now in Georgetown, was built next door. The decision had to be made without delay; and almost felt like a matter of national pride. Among Latin American diplomatic missions accredited to the White House, Venezuela, Haiti and Paraguay were the only ones without their own seat. Thus, the Venezuelan delegation, at this time without embassy rank, had been operating out of an apartment on 16th Street.

The foyer is a meeting point for all the main spaces.

The amplitude of spaces and the confluence of different atmospheres are typical of this residence.

After he decided upon the ideal spot on Massachusetts Avenue, Escalante forged ahead. There is a long letter from the envoy to the Foreign Ministry in Caracas reading, "A defect in the firmness of the ground…necessitated excavation work and the installation of concrete and steel pilasters," which forced him to make additional expenditures. The amount came to $ 21 204.23. The ambassador gave a detailed account of each item, and added, because perhaps it brought some consolation, that the neighboring Japanese embassy had spent over $50 000 on similar repairs. Moreover, he assured the Foreign Ministry in another missive that "Venezuela will have in Washington a magnificent ambassador's residence, very well located and original in its design. And all for a lesser investment than that which was made in the Pavilion at the New York's World's Fair."

A novel idea to remedy the lack of closet space was to excavate an underground room beneath the vestibule for the storage of coats and hats. These would go up and down in two small elevators operated by hand with an ingenious system of pulleys. This method had been used in London's Savoy Hotel with great success. The formula was copied and with such good results that it is still in use today in the Venezuelan ambassador's residence.

Nevertheless, not all of Escalante's requests were so well received. The copies painted by the talented D'Empayre remained in the residence until 1968, when they were replaced, little by little, by such works as Pedro Centeno's "The Three Races." This painting is a portrait of three nudes representing Venezuela's ethnic diversity, and was unearthed from the basement by an ambassador's wife. This is not the case with the bust of Bolívar that still

A tetralogy by the well-known Venezuelan artist Angel Hurtado hangs in the dining room. In the salon that leads to the dining room there are works by famous Venezuelan artists: Manuel Cabré, Brandt, Golding and González.

stands tall in one of the principal salons of the mansion. In time, as is natural, new initiatives were undertaken to provide greater comfort for guests and hosts. In 1965 a solarium and a pool were added. Despite some changes here and there, there is no doubt that this 20-room residence, one of the few expressly built as an embassy residence, still bears the seal of individuality and modernity that was dreamt of from day one. Ambassador Escalante would have been pleased.

Left
There is a fusion between the English and Italian style furnishings, with paintings by some 20th century Venezuelan artists, such as Armando Reverón and Héctor Poleo.

Above
One of the two wings of the staircase, in a distinctive Art déco style.

BIBLIOGRAPHY

Fiell, Charlotte and Peter. *Design of the 20th Century.*

Gómez Sicre, José. *Tiempo y Color. 16 pintores de Panamá.* Caracas, Venezuela: Litoven/ Ex Libris, 1991.

Hagströmer, Denise. *Swedish Design.* Stockholm: The Swedish Institute.

Highsmith, Carol M., and Ted Landphair. *Embassies of Washington*. Washington, D.C.: The Preservation Press, 1992.

Loeffler, Jane C. *The Architecture of Diplomacy: Building America's Embassies.* (New York: Princeton Architectural Press, 1998).

Miscelánea Antropológica Ecuatoriana. Boletín de los Museos del Banco Central – Año 1, No.1, 1981

Moreno Proaño, Agustín.*Tesoros Artísticos* - Museo Filanbanco. Guayaquil, 1983.

Ridings Miller, Hope. *Embassy Row. The Life and Times of Diplomatic Washington.* United States and Canada, Holt, Rinehart and Winston, 1969.

Scott, Pamela, and Antoinette J. Lee. *Buildings of the District of Columbia*. New York: Oxford University Press, 1993.

The U.S. Commission of Fine Arts. *Massachusetts Avenue Architecture*. 2 vols. Prepared by J. L. Sibley Jennings, Jr., Sue A. Kohler, and Jeffrey R. Carson. Washington, D.C.: Government Printing Office, 1973-75.

The U.S. Commission of Fine Arts. *Sixteenth Street Architecture*. 2 vols. Prepared by Sue A. Kohler and Jeffrey R. Carson. Washington, D.C.: Commission of Fine Arts, 1978-88.

Weeks, Christopher, for the Washington Chapter of the American Institute of Architects. *The AIA Guide to the Architecture of Washington, D.C.* Baltimore: The Johns Hopkins University Press, 1994.

See also websites associated with individual embassies and pamphlets and press materials available from the various embassies.

ACKNOWLEDGEMENTS

ARGENTINA, Dzidza de Amadeo and Eduardo Amadeo (present).

    Diego Ramiro Guelar (previous).

AUSTRIA, Elizabeth Moser Kahr and Dr. Peter Moser.

BELGIUM, Christiane van Daele and Frans van Daele (present).

    Rita Reyn and Alex Reyn (previous).

BOLIVIA, Pamela de Aparicio and Jaime Aparicio (present).

    Moira Valdés and Alberto Valdés (previous).

BRAZIL, María Ignez Barbosa and Rubens Barbosa.

CANADA, Margarita Fuentes and Michael Kergin.

CHILE, Lily Urdinola and Andrés Bianchi.

COLOMBIA, Gabriela Febres-Cordero and Luis Alberto Moreno.

DENMARK, Brigitte Hartnack Federspiel and Ulrik Federspiel.

ECUADOR, Anne de Gangotena and Raul Gangotena (present).

    Rocío de Jativa and Carlos Jativa (previous) Chargé d' Affaires, a.i.(previous).

    Ivonne A-Baki (previous).

EUROPEAN COMMISSION, Rita Byl Burghardt and Guenter Burghardt.

FRANCE, Marie-Cecile Levitte and Jean-David Levitte (present).

    Ann Bujon and Francois V. Bujon de L'Estang (previous).

GERMANY, Jutta Falke-Ischinger and Wolfgang Ischinger (present).

    Magda Gohar Chrobog and Wolfgang Friedrich Ischinger (previous).

GUATEMALA, Antonio Arenales Forno (present).

    Marta Marina Muñoz de Rivera and Ariel Rivera Irias (previous).

HOLY SEE, The Most Reverend Gabriele Montalvo.

ICELAND, Heba Augustsson and Helgi Augustsson (present).

    Brindis Schram and Jon Baldvin Hannibalsson (previous).

INDIA, Indira Mansing and Lalit Mansing.

INDONESIA, Suharti Brotodiningrat and Soemadi Brotodiningrat.

ITALY, Magda Vento and Sergio Vento (present).

    Anna Maria Salleo and Ferdinando Salleo (previous).

JAPAN, Hanayo Kato and Ryozo Kato (present).

    Shunji Yanai (previous).

KUWAIT, Rima Al-Sabah and Sheikh Salem Al-Jaber Al-Sabah (present).

    Ahmad Bader Mahmood Razouqui (previous).

LEBANON, Reem Abboud and Farid Abboud.

MEXICO, María Marcela Sánchez de Bremer and Juan Bremer.

MOROCCO, Maria Felice Cittadini Cesi and Azis Mekouar (present).

       Katheene El Maaroufi and Abdallah El Maaroufi, Azaze Makware (previous).

NORWAY, Ellen Sofie Aa. Vollebaek and Knut Vollebaek.

PANAMA, Rossana Ameglio de Alfaro and Roberto Alfaro Estripeaut (present).

       María del Pilar González Ruiz and Guillermo Alfredo Ford (previous).

PERU, Pauline Beck de Dañino and Roberto Dañino (present).

       Claudio de la Puente (previous).

       Julia Wagner and Alan Wagner (previous).

PORTUGAL, Cheryl Catarino and Pedro Catarino (present).

       Ana Rocha Paris and João Rocha Paris (previous).

ROMANIA, Carmen Ducaru and Dumitru Ducaru.

RUSSIA, Svetlana M. Ushakova and Yury Ushakov.

SINGAPORE, Chan Heng-Chee.

SOUTH AFRICA, Mathokoza Nhlapo and Thandabantu Nhlapo (present).

       Makate Sheila Sisulu (previous).

SPAIN, Rakela de Ruperez and Javier Ruperez.

SWEDEN, Kesrtin Eliasson and Jan Eliasson.

THE NETHERLANDS, Jellie van der Steeg and Boudewijn van Eenennaam (present).

       Yvonne Vos and Joris M. Vos (previous).

       Thomas Aquino Samodra Sriwidjaja (previous).

THE PEOPLE'S REPUBLIC OF CHINA, Aimei Le and Jiechi Yang (present).

       Quin Xiao Mei and Jiechi Yang.

THE REPUBLIC OF KOREA, Yi Song Mi and Han Joo (present).

       Jung Jin Lee Yang and Sung Chul Yang (previous).

TUNISIA, Faika Atallah and Hatem Atallah.

TURKEY, Mevhibe Logoglu and O. Faruk Logoglu (present).

       Baki Ilkin (previous).

UNITED KINGDOM, Lady Catherine and David Manning.

VENEZUELA, Margarete de Alvarez and Bernardo Alvarez Herrera (present).

       María de Herrera and Luis Herrera Marcano (previous).

COLLABORATORS

LUIS ALBERTO MORENO was designated Colombian Ambassador to the United States by Colombian President Andrés Pastrana in 1998 and his appointment to that post was ratified by the current President, Álvaro Uribe in 2002. Ambassador Moreno has presided over a notable improvement in the bilateral relations between Colombia and the United States. His work was decisive for the renovation and extension of the Andean Tariff Preferences Act. Before being named Ambassador he had a distinguished career in the Colombian private and public sectors. Between 1991 and 1994 he held important public posts, among them Minister of Economic Development in the administration of President César Gaviria, when he modernized the Ministry and its agencies with the aim of realizing a series of initiatives for the liberalization of the Colombian market. He was also president of the Institute of Industrial Promotion (Instituto de Fomento Industrial, "IFI"), the principal government financial corporation of Colombia and owner of some of the country's largest state companies. Under his leadership the Institute carried out an energetic program of privatization and developed new credit lines for different Colombian industries.

Ambassador Moreno obtained a degree in Business Administration and Economy from Florida Atlantic University and a MBA from Thunderbird University. He also studied at Harvard University on a Neiman scholarship.

As wife of the Ambassador of Colombia to the United States, GABRIELA FEBRES-CORDERO DE MORENO is a member of the board of directors of BellSouth-Colombia and an advisor to the Cuba-Policy Foundation in Washington, D.C. A graduate of the University of San Francisco, she has been president of the World Trade Center, Caracas, as well as a member of the board of directors of the World Trade Center Association, New York. Between 1989 and 1991, she was appointed to the cabinet position of Trade Representative of Venezuela, serving under the administration of President Carlos Andrés Pérez.

LILY URDINOLA DE BIANCHI is a Colombian journalist married to Andrés Bianchi, current Ambassador of Chile to the United States. Ms. Urdinola began her journalism studies in Italy (Prodeo) in 1964. In 1986 she continued them at the University of Chile in Santiago, where she graduated Summa Cum Laude in 1991. She has published numerous articles and interviews in such publications as the "Caras" magazine and "La Segunda" newspaper of Chile, and the newspaper "El País", in Cali, Colombia, and the Colombian magazine "Cromos."

ANTONIO CASTAÑEDA-BURAGLIA was born in Bogotá in 1947. He studied photography and film restoration at the Rochester Institute of Technology, N.Y., U.S.A. and did further studies at the Service National des Archives du Film, Bois D'Arcy, France. He has specialized in architecture and interior design. His publications include: *Anuario de la Arquitectura en Colombia* (Yearbook of Colombian Architecture, vols. 2,3,4,5,6,7,8,9,10) and *Testimonio de la Sociedad Colombiana de Arquitectura* (Record of the Colombian Society of Architecture). He has participated in the following books of Villegas Editores: *Museos de Bogotá* (Museums of Bogotá), *Casa Colombiana* (The Colombian House), *Casa Campesina* (The Peasant-Farmer House), *Casa Republicana* (The Republican House), *Casa Moderna* (The Modern House), *Casa de Hacienda* (The Hacienda House), *Casas Presidenciales* (Presidential Houses), *Palacio de Garzas* (Las Garzas Palace). Other works of his are *Ambientes Propios* (Their Own Ambiances) and *Un Mejor Modo de Vivir* (A Better Way of Living). His photographs (accompanied, at times, by articles) have been published in the magazines *DECORA* and *Semana* and in the newspaper *El Tiempo*. He was the restorer for the exhibition "History of Photography in Colombia", at the Bogotá Museum of Modern Art in 1983. He has exhibited in Colombia and abroad. He was awarded the Colombian Photography Prize in 2002.

JANE C. LOEFFLER is an architectural historian in Washington, D.C., and a visiting associate professor in the Honors Program at the University of Maryland, College Park. She is the author of *The Architecture of Diplomacy: Building America's Embassies* (1998) and numerous articles on U.S. government buildings in foreign countries. For her contributions to international affairs, the U.S. Department of State awarded her its Distinguished Public Service Award in 1998. A graduate of Wellesley College, Dr. Loeffler holds a Master's in City Planning from Harvard's Graduate School of Design and a Ph.D. in American Civilization from the George Washington University. For many years, she was associated with Frederick Gutheim, Washington planner and preservationist, and she has worked as a consultant to the National Gallery of Art and the National Building Museum. Her publications also include the introduction to Ezra Stoller's *United Nations* (1999) and articles and book reviews on topics ranging from landscape history to security and its impact on the design of public buildings.

PATRICIA CEPEDA is an interpreter and translator. She earned her B.A. in Comparative Literature cum laude from Yale and has done graduate work in Latin American Literature. For the three years that her husband John O'Leary served as U. S. Ambassador to Chile for Presidents Clinton and Bush, she lived in the U.S. Embassy residence in Santiago designed by Seattle architect Paul Thiry, the architect of the International Fair of Seattle.

While in Chile she organized, under the auspices of the State Department's "Art In the Embassies" program, the acclaimed exhibit "Maine Light" in the ambassador's residence, along with an extensive program of lectures and events. She and Ambassador O'Leary now live in Washington, D.C. and Little Diamond Island, Maine. They have two daughters, Alejandra and Gabriela.

Ambassador WALTER L. CUTLER. As a career diplomat in the United States Foreign Service, Walter Cutler served twice as Ambassador to The Kingdom of Saudi Arabia. He was also Ambassador to Tunisia and Zaire, and Ambassador-designate to Khomeni's Iran before diplomatic relations were broken. Other postings included Vietnam, Korea, Algeria and Cameroon. He currently directs Meridian International Center, a Washington-based educational and cultural institution dedicated to promoting global understanding through the exchange of people, ideas and the arts. He is a graduate of Wesleyan University and The Fletcher School of International Law and Diplomacy.

ISABEL CUTLER, a widely published photographer, has spent a large part of the last 20 years living & traveling in the Middle East. Her photographic portraits & landscapes are in Embassies and offices throughout the world, as well as in many private collections. The subjects of her portraits include prominent statesmen, artists and authors, as well as many other individuals, ranging from royal families in their palaces to neighborhood children in intimate family surroundings. She has been commissioned by the governments of Spain, Qatar & Kuwait to photograph their countries, and has held numerous exhibitions throughout the United States and in the Middle East & North Africa.

Cutler's work has appeared in such publications as *Architectural Digest*, *Vanity Fair*, and *Newsweek*, and her book "Mysteries of the Desert" was published by Rizzoli International Publications in 2001. She lives and maintains a studio in Washington, D.C.

BENJAMÍN VILLEGAS. An architect and graphic designer, he started publishing newspapers, books and magazines in the 1960's. In 1972 he founded Benjamín Villegas & Asociados and began to publish his large-format illustrated books of a high quality, while carrying on his work in graphic design, films and TV. In 1985 he created Villegas Editores, and exclusively devoted himself to publishing illustrated books by outstanding writers and photographers, with an emphasis on Colombia and the sponsorship of important public and private companies. At present, while still focussed on Colombia, he is carrying out publishing projects in several Latin American and European countries. Villegas Editores is the direct distributor of the Spanish versions of these books, while English versions are available worldwide through the catalogue of Rizzoli International, New York, and French versions through the catalogue of Vilo Difusion, Paris. His web-site – VillegasEditores.com – aims at making his books available to readers all over the world, winning support for the republication of those no longer in print, and strengthening his firm´s status as a leading publisher in Latin America. His original illustrated books surpass 150 titles, many of which have won important international awards. The quality and diversity of these books make them a unique literary and graphic collection. Mr. Villegas is recognized for having achieved the mission he set himself: showing the positive face of Colombia.